Pagans and Practitioners

SERIES VII
THEOLOGY AND RELIGION

VOL. 266

PETER LANG
New York • Washington, D.C./Baltimore • Bern
Frankfurt • Berlin • Brussels • Vienna • Oxford

Alf H. Walle

Pagans and Practitioners

Expanding Biblical Scholarship

PETER LANG
New York • Washington, D.C./Baltimore • Bern
Frankfurt • Berlin • Brussels • Vienna • Oxford

Library of Congress Cataloging-in-Publication Data

Walle, Alf H.
Pagans and practitioners: expanding biblical scholarship / Alf H. Walle.
p. cm. — (American university studies. VII, Theology and religion; v. 266)
Includes bibliographical references and index.
1. Bible. N.T.—Criticism, interpretation, etc. I. Title.
BS2361.3.W36   225.6—dc22   2009025956
ISBN 978-1-4331-0022-2
ISSN 0740-0446

Bibliographic information published by **Die Deutsche Nationalbibliothek**.
Die Deutsche Nationalbibliothek lists this publication in the "Deutsche
Nationalbibliografie"; detailed bibliographic data is available
on the Internet at http://dnb.d-nb.de/.

The paper in this book meets the guidelines for permanence and durability
of the Committee on Production Guidelines for Book Longevity
of the Council of Library Resources.

This volume of essays is dedicated to Loyd Melton and his broad
vision of *Biblical* scholarship. Melton has been my teacher and friend who
helped me explore the field of Biblical criticism and what it offers to both the
religious and the secular communities. My efforts would not have been
possible without Melton's help and encouragement.

Contents

Reframing Intellectual Connections

The purpose of this volume is to demonstrate how *Biblical* scholarship can be set upon a stronger foundation by affirming a solid and synergistic relationship with members of the larger intellectual community.

And vice versa.

The resulting collaboration is badly needed in order for (1) *Biblical* scholarship to embrace a wider range of ideas and concepts (2) while giving back to the larger academic world. We, a specialized discipline, must move in both directions in order to stand as full intellectual partners within the world of research, scholarship, and letters.

I am an interested outsider within Biblical studies: a role that possesses both strengths and weaknesses. I hope that these essays portray a useful vision of how the field can grow through fruitful collaboration with others.

Foreword

Maintaining a Focus

I come to *Biblical* research as an outsider. Nonetheless, I am a writer and teacher with scholarly experience and success in other disciplines including mythology (broadly defined) and the practitioner fields of business and human services. Hence, the title reads in part "Pagans and Practitioners." This background gives me a reasonable understanding of the intellectual world and the issues involved with it.

My previous publications include essays and books on how sacred and spiritual phenomena can be of service to fields such as social work and counseling as well as how certain causes (such as ecology) often function in ways that closely parallel conventional religion. I have even contributed essays on the *New Testament* that serve other fields, such as business and marketing. Thus, while my life's work has not taken place within a department of religious studies, linkages do exist.

My perspectives regarding *Biblical* scholarship began to expand in 2003 when I started taking post-doctoral graduate courses in *Biblical* studies at the Erskine Theological Seminary, working primarily with Loyd Melton, a *New Testament* specialist. I have done so as a respectful and sympathetic interloper who is aware of his limitations while realizing that my distinct background may, simultaneously, provide insights that others have, perhaps, overlooked. Although the sampling of coursework I have taken at seminary has not transformed me into a full fledged *Biblical* scholar, I have gained an appreciation for the field and its strengths, challenges, and concerns. I have also come to envision the contributions that *Biblical* scholarship is prepared to make to the larger intellectual community. In this spirit, I present the following essays. I hope that my distance from *Biblical* scholarship (even when working within the field) proves to be an asset and not a liability.

Disciplines need to both borrow from the greater scholarly world and contribute to it. Some fields, for whatever reason, have taken significantly more than they have given. These "recipient disciplines" can easily be judged as "second class citizens" of the scholarly world. When these fields begin to give back, however, they emerge on a par with their peers. Full partnership status, of course, should be a goal of every discipline, *Biblical* scholarship included.

It appears to me that, for a variety of reasons, contemporary *Biblical* scholarship comes close to fitting the mold of a "recipient discipline" and, therefore, its status and influence within the greater scholarly community might be somewhat undermined as a result. That is the bad news. The good news is that things do not have to be that way. While *Biblical* scholarship has a specific universe of discourse, the tools it has developed and the insights it has gained can and should be shared with others. These "others" include both those who have a primary interest in some aspect of religion and those from more secular and practitioner-oriented fields.

A few years ago, I published two essays in the refereed management literature that deal with the *New Testament* what were designed to contribute to contemporary business thought. Both proved to be useful enough to be reprinted, among other places, in my book *Rethinking Marketing*. These successes have emboldened me to continue to merge Biblical criticism and other fields. Although there is much talk regarding how to use the principles of business and marketing within the context of religion, my thinking goes in the opposite direction and argues that a look at the *New Testament* can help members of the business community to better understand their work and the issues they face.

The first essay entitled "The *Bible* of International Business" concerns the work of St. Paul and the attempts of his ministry to reach out to the gentile world. All *Biblical* scholars, of course, are familiar with Paul and the rivalry that existed between him and the Judiazers who believed that Christianity was an offshoot of Judaism, a situation that required all believers to embrace Jewish laws and traditions. The tensions between these two views provided me with the opportunity to discuss an issue of profound importance within contemporary business thought: the ongoing debate regarding the degree to which the firm should market products in a single way to the entire world vs. adjusting the product to mesh with the demands and expectations of specific markets. I praised Paul as a man who understood the value of envisioning a product in its most basic form while strategically tailoring the presentation so it jived with the predispositions, preferences, and cultural traditions of each distinct target market.

The business disciplines tend to praise the advances they have made in dealing with the complexities of a global economy. My essay, in contrast, demonstrates that 2000 years ago decision makers were keenly aware of and hotly debated the exact issues that concern today's "innovative" strategists. By presenting the example of Paul's work, I was able to document that his responses reveal timeless and universal strategies that are not merely an artifact of our era. By doing so, false beliefs regarding the alleged distinctiveness of today's world are forcefully challenged.

The second essay "The Positioning of Good News" dealt with the four gospels as examples of marketing communications. (i.e. early efforts at advertising and public relations.) The key principle of marketing is the "marketing concept" that argues that the sole purpose of an organization is to serve its customers. As a result, the demands of specific target markets need to be addressed in ways that are tailored to their needs and desires. Following this dictate, marketing communications are tailored to the needs and expectations of specific audiences.

The situation was portrayed by comparing differences in the four gospels. Each was analyzed using a covert and unstated form of "redaction criticism" in order to show that specific writers presented their messages in ways that would impress specific groups of people. While Mark wrote a general and largely non-strategic document, The Gospel of *Matthew* catered to the Jewish community while the *Gospel of John* was phrased in ways to which the Hellenistic community could more easily respond.

While *Mark*, *Matthew*, and *John* were addressed to "end users" or "customers", the *Gospel of Luke* can be viewed as a public relations document that was aimed at members of the Roman civil service. The author of *Luke* wrote during a lull of persecution after the horrors inflicted by Nero. The threat of further reprisals, however, continued to exist. By presenting Christianity in ways that dispelled the notion that the church was a threat to the Roman state, Luke, in effect, lobbied for less hostile treatment by governmental officials.

Like "the Bible of International Business", the "Positioning of Good News" has been recognized precisely because it contributed to the scholarly discussions of marketing in positive and productive ways through the use of Biblical examples. For our purposes, the reception of these two essays demonstrates that, under certain circumstances, *Biblical* scholarship can provide insights to the larger intellectual community and to the practitioner realm. Certainly, marketing is contributing to religious activities by helping churches to function in a more effective manner through the embrace of useful strategies and tactics. While this is true, Biblical scholarship is also a part of a conversation that has ultimately resulted in members of the business community rethinking their own orientations. Thus, *Biblical* scholarship is not merely a recipient discipline that takes much while giving little back. It, in contrast, is a part of the larger intellectual community and provides useful perspectives to it.

While *Biblical* scholarship, as shown above, has the ability to contribute to the larger community, it often uses the ideas of others to achieve its goals. In the second cluster of essays, the value of nesting *Biblical* scholarship within a larger framework of the social and spiritual milieu of the Roman Empire is discussed. *Biblical* researchers, of course, have long done so and this pre-existing scholarly underpinning provides a foundation for my work. It is acknowledged and appreciated.

In these essays, the focus is much more centered upon pagan religions and ancient philosophies than is often the case. Christianity is interpreted from within this context. By looking at ancient spiritual and religious systems on their own terms and from a somewhat sympathetic perspective, Christianity is discussed in an increasingly robust manner.

In Chapter 3, the "Three Marys and Mithras", the depiction of the gambling soldiers at the cross as it appears in the *Gospel of John* is reexamined. Scholars typically assume that John's treatment of this episode is an inadvertent and non-strategic rephrasing of the synoptic gospels. That popular premise is challenged by showing that John's rendition presents the gambling soldiers in a way that replicates the tension between the early church and the cult of Mithras. In view of the fact that the cult of Mithras was viewed as a strong rival to Christianity, this comparison allowed the author(s) of *John* to make important theological allusions that have hitherto gone unnoticed by modern scholars. In making this case, the essay deals with the tensions between the early church and the pagan world that, otherwise, would not be adequately addressed.

In Chapter 4, *Luke's* parable of the "Rich Fool" is interpreted as a rather pointed critique of Epicurean philosophy. Doing so goes beyond the usual interpretations that view the parable as a commentary on exemplary behavior, etc. By comparing *Luke's* version with a parallel account that appears in the *Gospel of Thomas*, it can be shown that the author of Luke took a generic parable about stewardship and greed and transformed it into a hostile and pointed appraisal of a specific philosophy that was at odds with Christian belief. Epicureanism, furthermore, was in conflict with stoicism, a philosophy and ethical foundation largely associated with the Roman civil service. In view of the fact that the author of *Luke* wrote, in part, to impress Roman decision makers who were in a position to extend more favorable treatment to the church, this tactic was important. Thus, by critiquing Epicureanism, Luke finds fault with a philosophy that rivals Christianity while simultaneously helping the church reach out to the Roman civil service by affirming that they collectively oppose a common foe.

In Chapter 5 "Christianity, Bacchus, and Sexual License", the *Epistle of Jude* is reexamined with reference to the religious context of the ancient world. *Jude* tends to be dismissed as a generic call to oppose false teachers (whoever they may be) and, as such, it is not given much theological weight by *Biblical* scholars. Indeed, *Jude* has long been lumped with the "catholic letters" that are assumed to deal with general issues, not specific threats that faced distinct congregations at a specific point in history.

The treatment of *Jude* provided here, in contrast, suggests that the author was concerned with a very distinct threat facing a specific congregation: the desire of advocates of the cult of Bacchus to merge with Christianity and rework the church for its own purposes. This proposed merging was facilitated by the fact that certain inadvertent similarities between Christ and Bacchus exist. The counter attack presented in *Jude*, furthermore, resonates from aspects of the cult of Bacchus that *Biblical* scholars have not noticed. Once these clues are recognized, however, the epistle's specific point of reference becomes obvious. Unfortunately, because it has not been viewed from within this context, *Jude* has often been trivialized by the scholarly community.

While chapters 3 though 5 focus upon how to more fully nest *Biblical* scholarship within the context of the ancient world, chapters 6 and 7 present *Biblical* scholarship as a discipline that has much to contribute to the current intellectual and practitioner scene that exists today.

In Chapter 6, "Form Criticism and Native Ecology" the ability of form criticism to serve within a wider context is discussed. Form critics seek to deal with the fact that the oral tradition can impact the way in which information is remembered and passed on to the next generation. As a result, seminal scholars such as Rudolph Bultman have dealt with the synoptic gospels from this perspective. Many other disciplines, such as folklore, also deal with the oral tradition and its impacts. Much of this heritage has sacred, spiritual, and religious significance. This raises the question: can the techniques advocated by Bultman et al be adapted to the study of folklore and oral history? If so, can Biblical scholarship contribute these analytic tools to the larger intellectual community?

While Chapter 6 deals with scholarly work, Chapter 7, "Parables within the Framework of Recovery", deals with practitioner issues. The *New Testament*, although a sacred text, can often be put to use by practitioners. In some circumstances, furthermore, the sacred nature of the *New Testament* may provide it with a power that secular documents lack. This is dramatized by showing how the parables of Jesus can be reworked in ways that help substance abuse counselors to more effectively serve their clients. By doing so, the case is made that *Biblical* scholars may have a role in helping others to more effectively function within their professions. Thus, *Biblical* scholars, besides functioning within their own discipline are in a position to help both scholars and practitioners from other fields.

While this book revolves around a general theme (expanding the scope of *Biblical* scholarship) it is, of course, a reflection of the author's personal background, interests, experiences, and taste. As a result, the suggestions made here are suggestive, idiosyncratic, and not exhaustive. It is hoped that others who are committed to advancing the discipline of *Biblical* studies will, in their own ways, demonstrate the vitality and relevance of their field in the work they do.

Part 1

Redaction Criticism in a New Key

Prologue to Part 1 (Chapters 1 and 2)

Redaction Criticism in a New Key

The first two chapters in this book do not have the look and feel of Biblical scholarship because, in the final analysis, they are not.

While I have always been interested in religious topics, my work in the field was an avocation until 2003 when I began to take post-doctoral graduate courses in theology (at the Erskine Theological Seminary in Due West, South Carolina.) Nonetheless, over the years, I have used examples from Christianity when writing in other disciplines. In doing so, I have sought to provide a broader perspective to the business disciplines. The first two chapters of this book are examples of doing so.

A few years ago, I published versions of Chapters 1 and 2 within the refereed business literature in order to demonstrate that many of the strategic tools "innovated" by contemporary marketing were overtly used by ancient strategists. While many business scholars and practitioners (suffering from the sin of hubris) congratulate themselves for inventing the techniques they champion, the tools they showcase are, in reality, "so old they are new again."

In order to demonstrate this fact, I applied modern business theories to the four gospels and to the life of Saint Paul. While offbeat within the business literature, the articles were warmly embraced, widely praised, and been republished both in journals and as part of one of my books *Rethinking Marketing*. The reception these essays received is proof that the significance of this kind of analysis is valued by the business community.

The basic theme of these two essays is that those who wrote (and walk through) the *New Testament* were strategic individuals who carefully planned what they said and did in order to effectively present their message to specific target markets. As a result, the literary tactics of these early Christian leaders can be envisioned with reference to modern marketing strategies.

Bedrock ideas of business (such as the" marketing concept" and "total quality management") implore leaders to embrace customers as they actually exist and to devise strategies that will attract them. These orientations can be applied to both for-profit and not-for-profit organizations.

Today, of course, pastors often seek advice on how to use the consumer-oriented theories that were developed within business in order to attract and serve a congregation. The success of the Willow Creek Community Church, under the direction of Bill Hybels, is a good example of how modern marketing methods can help a church to achieve its goal. Hybels conducted a door-to-door survey in Great Barrington, Illinois in order to learn why people did not attend church (Willow Creek Community Church History, 2005.) After analyzing the results of this research, the church implemented various changes in order to better respond to the desires and needs of the community. Attendance and membership shot up. Hybels clearly recognized that successfully serving people is largely hinged upon responding to their habits, expectations, and needs. (This, of course, was also the policy of St. Paul during the early days of the church when he advocated ministering to gentiles on their own terms.) The success of the Willow Creek Community Church is a classic example of applying the marketing concept (a customer-oriented business orientation) in order to make a church more effective.

The underlying principle of the marketing concept affirms that since organizations exist to serve clients (or potential clients), strategies and tactics must take their needs, feelings, and expectations into account when serving them. Thus, to be effective, organizations and the tools they use (such as a promotional literature) must be strategically adjusted to those being served.

As Chapters 1 and 2 demonstrate, this perspective was not invented in the late 20th century. For thousands of years, people have (overtly or covertly) understood the value of applying customer-oriented strategies. As we shall see, the *New Testament* provides concrete examples of such strategic thought that date back 2000 years.

Ultimately the basic principles and orientations of redaction criticism can be used to make the same basic point as the marketing concept because both concepts acknowledge that those who communicate tend to adjust their message with a specific target audience in mind. Redaction criticism emphasizes that the strategic goals of authors cannot be totally ignored (even though some *Biblical* scholars might rebut this premise using what has been called "intentional fallacy.")

When I created the first versions of Chapters 1 and 2, I was not aware of redaction criticism. As a result, these essays, although written by someone interested in the *New Testament*, were not influenced by modern trends in Biblical scholarship. Having immersed myself in formal Biblical scholarship in recent years, I now see linkages between redaction criticism and my earlier analysis of the *New Testament*.

When revising these materials, I could have more fully incorporated techniques such as redaction criticism to make may work better reflect modern Biblical scholarship. After considering that option, I decided to let these documents stand essentially as originally written, introducing only modest changes. Thus, while the essays offered here may seem to be a little out of step and not fully in sync with the prevailing *Biblical* literature, I hesitate to "put old wine in new skins." This strategy has the benefit of presenting a chain of thought in a streamlined form that is easy to understand (and hopefully is entertaining.) I hope that this method of presentation serves the reader well.

References

Willow Creek Community Church, (2005.) Willow creek community church history. Retrieved Dec. 1, 2005, from Willow Creek Community Church Web site: http://www.willowcreek.org/history.asp>.

Chapter 1

The *Bible* of International Business

The first two chapters of this book deal, in some detail, with events that are chronicled in the *New Testament*. While these topics have been visited by innumerable scholars, my treatment is distinctive because it is based on modern management thought. Originally, versions of these essays were published within the secular, business literature to demonstrate that the strategies currently used by business were consciously employed 2000 years ago. The discussion that takes place here (in Chapter 1), deals primarily with the work of Saint Paul and his ministry. Chapter 2 compares the four gospels in order to show how specific texts were crafted to most effectively influence the specific target market being addressed

I have resisted the temptation to reformulate these chains of thought to reflect modern *Biblical* scholarship. By preserving the original form of these essays, they present a useful commentary with a minimum of diversions and jargon. It is hoped that any limitations the reader may sense will be accepted as rhetorical devices inherent in the business case study format.

Peter and the Rise of Ethnic Niching

After Jesus Christ withdrew from active, day to day, participation in his organization, Simon (also known as St. Peter), emerged as the CEO. Peter typifies both the strengths and weaknesses of executives who are apt to assume leadership when the founder of an innovative new firm moves on. Peter's credentials did not stem from his strategic prowess, but resulted from long-term involvement in the organization. He was well connected and possessed a dominant personality. His nickname "The Rock" was given to him by Christ who seemingly believed that the emerging leadership of the church would build upon his strength (*Matthew* 16:18.) A former entrepreneur who previously managed a small family-centered commercial fishing business (*Mark* 1: 16), Peter undoubtedly possessed the skills required to supervise "rank and file" subordinates and to oversee the day-to-day operations of a small, localized operation. Apparently an ambitious "fast tracker", Peter welcomed managerial opportunities; after the defection of Judas Iscariot, who had been bribed into revealing important secrets to competitors, Peter assumed leadership and named a replacement (*Acts* 1: 1 5–23.) Familiar with the current status of the organization and the uncontrollable variables that had to be faced domestically, Peter was effective, especially at a local level.

In addition, Peter was an excellent salesman when communicating with local Jews; in one day's preaching he recruited approximately 3,000 new clients (*Acts*, Chapter 2).

A man with significant skills, Peter also possessed profound limitations that could become crippling if he attempted to move his locally-oriented firm towards multinational status. Being raised in the village of Bethesda in Galilee, Peter was rather provincial and he lacked the worldly sophistication required to transform the church from a Jewish splinter-group into a multinational organization. Certainly, Peter may have known Greek (the "lingua Franca" of his era) to a limited degree, but he could hardly have been fluent, especially in the early days of his administration. Biblical scholars, for example, often doubt that Peter actually authored *1 Peter* because it is written in excellent Greek, a language that Peter, a small-town fisherman, probably had not mastered to that degree of sophistication.

Although Peter lacked the ability to function effectively outside Palestine, he, nonetheless, believed that the mission of his organization transcended the needs of his homeland and the traditions of Judaism; after all, Christ had dealt with gentiles (*John* 12:20–36): evidence that the church was for all people and that it was not merely a Jewish sect. Peter's decision to "go international" is dramatized by the fact that he personally established the policy of allowing clients to become Christians without being required to observe traditions, laws, and mores that were uniquely Jewish.

Although such attitudes underscore Peter's multinational orientations, he apparently did not possess the ability to interact decisively outside the Jewish community; thus, the first gentile convert, Cornelius, was completely familiar with Palestinian culture and regularly attended Jewish religious services even before his conversion. Since this was the case, Cornelius was obviously able to interact meaningfully, with a small-town Jew, even though Peter's knowledge of Latin and Greek did not match that of a Roman sophisticate.

The situation during the early years of Peter's administration dramatizes his inability to establish a multinational thrust for his organization. A major faction called the Judaizers, for example, insisted that the church should position itself as Jewish organization that revolved around Hebrew beliefs and traditions. According to this perspective, gentile converts were required to embrace all Jewish laws and traditions (including circumcision and restrictive dietary laws.)

The Judaizers had several trump cards to play; all the influential apostles were devout Jews who routinely worshiped in Jewish temples even after

Christ's death (*Luke*, 24:53.) Christ, furthermore, stated that he hoped to fulfill Jewish traditions, not destroy them (*Matthew*, 5:17.) In the eyes of the Judaizers, Peter's conversion of Cornelius (as a gentile who was not required to embrace Jewish ways) was merely a random, isolated event and not a precedent-setting incident.

So strong was the influence of the Judaizers within the managerial elite of the early church that Peter, the CEO, began to feel that his position would be in jeopardy if he failed to follow their wishes. When visiting Antioch, for example, Peter acted contrary to his beliefs by holding himself aloof from gentile Christians and by refusing to eat or mingle with them; he choose this course of action because he feared the Judaizers (*Galatians*, 2:11–14.) Obviously, the Judaizers had gained such a sway over the management of the infant church that even the CEO was forced to compromise his ideals and shelve his international initiatives in order to stay in power.

Franchising, and Multinational Status

As we have seen, Peter initially favored a multinational strategy and he forcefully moved in that direction; eventually, however, he was intimidated into overtly contradicting his multinational priorities and ultimately bowed to a leadership that wanted to serve a specific target market: the Jewish community.

Unfortunately, the product being offered could not be shelved until some future time when the home office chose to broaden its strategies. Instead, a "strategic window", that momentarily offered opportunities for expansion, was beginning to close; Mithraism, a rival faith, was winning converts and quickly spreading throughout the Roman world. Although Christianity and Mithraism were different in many respects

> "... both religions were of Oriental origin; they were propagated about the same time, and spread with equal rapidity on account of the same causes, viz, the unity of the political world and the debasement of its moral life" (Showerman 1910 624.)

Besides providing a bundle of benefits that appealed to many gentiles, Mithraism had a method of organization that obviously surpassed the structure of the early Christian church that had been patched together by a handful of rural provincials who possessed scant knowledge of organizational theory. Mithraism, in contrast, was a religion popular among soldiers, who had a sense of organizational priorities, a vision of strategic action, and a hierarchy of command. Indeed the very name of the god, Mithras, means "contract" (Duchense-Guilleman 1967 982) and the religion was organized as a "legal corporation enjoying the right of holding property" (Showerman 1910 624.) Without doubt, Mithraism was a dangerous rival to Christianity, not only did it already control a significant share of the gentile market, it was organized as a property owning corporation and it was administered by executives with experience in the Roman Army, a finely tuned organization/bureaucracy. Not surprisingly, philosopher/historian E. R. Renan, among other scholars, suggests that the Roman world would have become Mithraic if it had not eventually turned Christian.

In short, a major crisis existed; the Jerusalem "home office" was in no position to "go international", but if concrete action were not taken immediately, the market would have become saturated with a rival product, a situation that would inhibit, if not curtail, future expansion. The sophisticated nature of Mithraism compounded the threat and dictated the need for immediate response.

Facing this sort of challenge, domestically oriented companies often grant franchises to outside individuals who possess the skills required to compete in the international arena. This, according to Christian tradition, is the strategy chosen by Jesus when he chose a manager for the international franchise. Christ, seemingly, used a technique common even today among corporate recruiters: he hired a highly skilled "player" who previously worked for a direct competitor. This tactic allows the recruiting company to acquire a seasoned "pro" who already understood the situation, requires little training to become effective, and (being a known personality within the industry) brought prestige and respectability to the struggling new organization.

Saul was such a candidate; his job prior to becoming international marketing manager for the church was to work with the traditional Jewish hierarchy in order to limit the market share of Christianity among people of Jewish origin. In this position, he was an inquisitor and persecutor of the emerging sect and he wielded considerable clout among "spies, temple soldiers, and legal authority" (Schroeder 1963 3.) In such a role, Saul understood the strategic situations to be faced in his new position and he undoubtedly possessed a wealth of inside information.

In accordance with typical "headhunting" tactics still used today, Christ interviewed Saul while he was traveling and could be consulted in private; at that meeting Christ suggested Saul should work for, not against, the new organization. According to the *Act of the Apostles*, (9 3–19) Christ used special effect presentations (a vision and a miracle) to underscore his recruitment pitch and Saul was eventually won over.

Christ established a franchise arrangement with Saul, who was to be responsible for introducing the church's product line to the gentiles and to members of the elite educated minority, a group that modern marketing recognizes as the innovating class (*Acts*, 9:15.)

As might be expected, opponents questioned the legitimacy of Saul's franchise arrangement; after all, it was based on an oral agreement made without witnesses. As a result, he was constantly portrayed as a second-rate apostle (Castelot 1967 14) by his rivals who explicitly referred to his weak links with the Jerusalem "home office." Saul, of course, responded that he had been given a franchise by Christ (owner of the product line) and, therefore, his authority did not need to stem from any other division of the corporation. Indeed, much of Saul's writing concerns claim and counter-claim regarding his authority (see *2 Corinthians* Chapters 10 to 13) Such internal rivalry is common even today when international franchises gain too much authority and/or act in a manner that is inconsistent with the established corporate strategy. Under such circumstances, franchises are often depicted as second-rate and/or at odds with the goals of the organization as a whole. Even when the franchise system is legitimized, certain members of the old guard (who lose clout as power shifts away from them) inevitably discount the success of the international division, since their own position may be undermined by the new state of affairs that is emerging.

Internal squabbles notwithstanding, Christ's choice of Saul as manager of the international franchise was an excellent strategy; not only did Saul have Jewish credentials that exceeded those of the church's existing management, he also possessed the worldly sophistication required to successfully mingle in international circles. Such abilities stem from the fact that Saul was both a pious Jew and a well educated Roman citizen. He was raised in the cosmopolitan Roman city of Tarsus; "a meeting place for East and West, a crossroad for commerce ... where the democratic traditions of the Greek city states has long been established" (Packer 1980 5.)

Descended from a family of devout Jewish leaders, Saul was extremely religious and habitually followed both the spirit and the letter of Jewish religious laws. Trained to be a Pharisee, he was knowledgeable in Jewish ways and possessed a vita full of enviable Jewish credentials. As such, he possessed the intellectual pedigree required to create an intellectual justification for his new organization. Saul had also mastered the interpersonal and strategic skills that were needed to counter the internal and external threats to the church as it went international.

The fact that Paul was a Jew of the Diaspora gave him the ability to function internationally. The Diaspora, the settlement of Jewish communities over a wide area of what was then the Roman world, had existed for hundreds of years and, as early as 55 BC, Cicero indicates some Jews of the Diaspora had become Roman citizens. Saul and his family were such people; they were Jewish while possessing Roman citizenship and all privileges related to it.

Being raised in Tarsus, a university town, Saul was familiar with both Greek and Roman culture and the lifestyles of various peoples scattered throughout the Empire. Being a Roman citizen, he was aware of Roman law and how it could be used to advantage; few domestic Palestinians could make that claim. Fluent in Greek and Latin, able to quote Greek poets, and to discuss professional athletics as an insider, Saul had a remarkable set of skills to offer a small domestically-oriented firm that sought to serve additional cultural groups.

No one who has ever worked in the international arena can doubt the wisdom of choosing Saul as an international representative. A member of the same general socio-ethnic group as the management of the domestic office he was not the type of man to completely "go native" which is always a factor to consider when choosing international representatives. Nevertheless, be exhibited the skills and the temperament that are essential when functioning as an equal in the internationally sphere.

In summary, during its early days, the church faced two sets of rivals. Domestically, Christianity was an innovation that found itself pitted against an entrenched Judaism. Many leaders of Christianity thought of themselves as part of the Jewish cultural tradition; as a result, they favored a strict "niching strategy" and concentrated upon the Jewish community.

As we have seen, however, the gentile market was in danger of being lost to Mithraism, a rival religion that was professionally managed, organized as a legal corporation, and provided a spiritual solution to many of the same pressures that Christianity alleviated.

During this phase, a franchise arrangement was appropriate since the home office was unable and/or unwilling to abandon a classic niching strategy, centered around the Jewish community. Nonetheless, the leader of the international franchise also needed a sophisticated understanding of the traditional (Jewish) market segment since this knowledge would be required for the eventual reintegration and unification of the domestic and the international divisions. The executive chosen to fulfill these dual responsibilities of expansion and reintegration was Saul, a devout Jew steeped in international experience.

The Rise of a Multinational

Saul was keenly aware that the key strategic decision in international marketing involves determining the degree to which a product should embrace the lifestyles of each unique target to be served. His tenure as international marketing manager was characterized by a profound ability to determine which characteristics of Christianity could be legitimately modified in order to respond to specific target markets. At the same time, however, this accommodation needed to be accomplished in ways that avoided undermining the essence of the organization. Saul's career is a textbook example of successfully crafting localized marketing strategies, aimed at specific targets, while applying them in tactical ways that did not undercut the core mission of the organization.

Paul's transcendence of strategies that were aimed solely at the Jewish subculture is best symbolized by the fact that, during his missionary journey, Saul used the name *Paul* which, being Roman, did not identify him and his organization with any specific ethnic group.

As might be expected, Paul/Saul abbreviated the demands of the organization to their very essence. He was concerned with winning clients and he had little interest in the specific details of how to accomplish his goal. In the classic essay, ""Marketing Myopia" business guru Theodore Levitt (1960) suggests that the downfall of the railroads stemmed directly from the perception that they were in the "railroad business" (a definition based on method and technique) and not in the "transportation business" (a definition based upon the actual services being rendered.) Because railroad executives historically viewed their business in narrow and circumscribed ways, significant opportunities (such as acquiring the infant air lines during the 1930s) were ignored. The lesson in Levitt's example is that those who focus on specifics may overlook the actual service being provided. When this happens the organization can easily suffer and decline.

Paul was well aware of the marketing truths that, in our era, have been rephrased in discussions, such as that found in "Marketing Myopia." In his quest to serve clients and win market share, Paul never confused the mission of his organization with the specifics of the immediate circumstance.

Paul possessed the ability to state the mission of his organization simply and concretely and pare away all distracting non-essentials. Doing so, Paul consciously expanded the number of possible target markets that his organization could effectively serve. He states, for example, that "there is no distinction between Jew and Greek, for the same Lord is lord of all" (*Romans*, 10: 12.) Asserting this, Paul consciously embraced a localized international marketing strategy that he believed was essential for growth. Paul, for example, observes, "Inasmuch as I am an apostle of gentiles, I magnify my ministry" (*Romans*; 11:13.) He then generalized and simplified the costs of becoming a client by merely requiring that: "Whosoever believes in Him [Christ] will not be disappointed ... Whoever will call upon the name of the Lord will be saved"

(*Romans*, 10:11–13.) Note that doing so did not require the embrace of Jewish lifestyles and customs.

The strategic significance of Paul's approach lies in the fact that it does not insist that new clients abandon their own traditions, habits, and preferences before joining the organization. As we have seen, before Paul's tenure Christians were expected to embrace all Jewish traditions, laws, and dietary customs. Without doubt, the biggest stumbling block to gentile conversion was circumcision which, according to the Judaizers, was required of all male Christians. This regulation, no doubt, resulted in significant "sales resistance" among adult non-circumcised gentile men. Abandoning this requirement, Paul removed a major obstacle of recruitment.

Paul, nonetheless, knew that he would be interacting with more conservative Christians who favored retaining Jewish ethnic traditions; as a result, he had Timothy, a fellow missionary and traveling companion, circumcised. This decision, seemingly contradictory to Paul's teachings, actually shows a profound strategic sense, "Paul knew how to fight for a principle and how to yield for expediency when no principle was at stake" (Packer 1980 554.)

Paul actually boasts of his chameleon nature and the positive effects it has on his sales presentation, observing, "To the weak I become weak, that I might win the weak; I have become all things to all men, that I may by all means [accomplish my organization's goals]" (*I Corinthians*, 9:22.)

Paul's sales techniques also demonstrate a profound ability to nest the product within the context of the local market he was cultivating. Paul, for example, felt comfortable working examples from Greek poets into his presentation (*Acts* 17:28.) Paul went so far as to overtly link Christ with the Greek pantheon of gods; at Mars Hill in Athens, Greece, for example, he noted that when "I was examining the objects of your worship, I also found an altar with this inscription, 'To an Unknown God' " (*Acts* 17:23.) The Greeks (who believed in many gods) realized that they might be unaware of some deities and, out of courtesy to them, had built a small shrine for any god or gods that may have been overlooked. A man who knew the value of launching products in terms that meshed with the world view of prospective clients, Paul proclaimed that he represented that "Unknown God". By doing so, he portrayed Christ as a God that the Greeks already acknowledged and linked Christ to the Hellenistic religious traditions: an excellent international strategy.

Traveling widely, Paul met with and wrote to people who were very different from him. Facing this situation, international promoters typically deal with human universals to which all people can respond regardless of their specific culture. Paul clearly embraced such promotional techniques, often drawing upon sports analogies to make his message universal.

In one letter, for example, Paul states that "forgetting what lies behind and straining forward to what lies ahead, I press towards the mark for the prize [of my religion]" (*Philippians* 3:13–14.) This is an obvious allusion to a footrace in which the professional athlete seeks money (a prize), speeds towards the finish line (mark), and knows that if he loses his power of concentration (looks back) he will fail (Wicks 1957 96.) Paul also uses terminology that translates "toil" and "strive" which in the original Greek were part "of the vocabulary of the games of track and field" (Wicks 1957 183.) Likewise, Paul refers to "laboring fervently for you"; the particular verb he chose originally referred to "contesting for the prizes in games of track and field" (Wicks 1957 238.)

Even more blatant are Paul's observations that "an athlete is not crowned unless he competes according to the rules" (2 *Timothy*, 2.5) and his eloquent assessment of his own life: "I have fought the good fight, I have finished the race" (2 *Timothy*, 4:7.)

Such examples are more than evidence that Paul was familiar with the international popular culture of his world; they also demonstrate that he was aware that athletics are a human universal, shared and enjoyed by all people. The historical fact that Rome had spread a number of sports throughout the known world enhanced the value of the athletic analogies Paul used. In our era, of course, firms such as Coca Cola often utilize sports motifs, examples, and spokespeople when promoting their products. The fact that a famous television commercial initially featuring "Mean Joe Green" was recreated using local sports heroes from many countries demonstrates the universality of athletics in international promotion. Paul, like Coca Cola, was well aware of this fact.

Besides simplifying and generalizing the product and marketing mix of the church (in a manner that that enabled many different peoples to emerge as potential clients), Paul also showed great skill in setting up franchises that, while independent, could simultaneously be integrated into a greater organizational network.

During the era of early international expansion, Paul embarked on three missionary journeys; together they show striking similarities to modern international marketers who work to extend the organization's range to new areas while maintaining close contact with an increasingly far-flung network of regional offices. During his first journey, Paul visited a number of cities in Asia Minor, set up local organizations, and then retraced his footsteps so that the majority of cities were visited twice. During the second journey, he revisited several key cities and expanded his market range to include Greece and parts of Palestine. During the third journey, he again went to cities earlier visited during his first two trips while also continuing to expand the organizational network that already existed. Today, we find the same strategy being employed by representatives of organizations who must skillfully divide their time between maintaining established accounts versus forging ahead to embrace virgin territory. Paul's epistles (inter-organizational correspondences) provided further communication between Paul and an increasingly dispersed franchise network.

Besides setting up franchises and providing periodic support services, Paul also built a degree of autonomy into local organizations. Each was headed by a regional manager (Presbyter), an executive with decision-making powers who had the authority to translate the tenets of the organization to mesh with local conditions. "The Presbyter by reason of his office ruled ... his community, corrected abuses, was vigilant against false teachers ... and was an authority, teacher and arbiter" (Chiovare 1967 746.) Thus, Paul set up largely independent franchises that possessed an ability to adjust the product line to meet local conditions. Simultaneously, Paul maintained personal contact, corresponded, and provided support services to individual franchises.

The resulting semi-autonomy probably gave Christianity a differential advantage over its chief rival, Mithraism, a religion that was strictly hierarchical in nature. Mithraism (as discussed above) was highly authoritarian; it offered an alternative to Roman decadence, but it demanded total adherence to the elite on the upper rungs of the organizational ladder. To overcome the "experience curve advantages" and "brand loyalty" already enjoyed by Mithraism, the struggling church desperately required uniqueness and distinctiveness; providing a degree of local autonomy was one way to do so. Autonomy both divorced the organization from the ethnocentrism of the Judaizers of the early Jerusalem church and made Christianity a distinctive alternative to Mithraism, an established rival. In this way, Paul's organization avoided being just another "me-too" product (a mere alternative to Mithraism) and offered unique advantages not hitherto available to the public.

In sum, Paul, a man with a wealth of international credentials, used his talents to the hilt when establishing the Christian church as a multinational organization. Virtually everything he did would satisfy the criteria of modern business methods as practiced by enlightened international firms. Paul provided the church with a degree of universality but, beyond these guidelines, individual franchises were allowed to adjust the product line to suit the temperament of the particular target being served. Giving freedom to regional managers (Presbyters), Paul used his missionary journeys and his written communications to keep in touch. In his evangelical work, Paul shows great skill in jockeying his time between existing franchises and new, untapped, markets.

Paul's successes, however, led to rivalries and tensions between his franchise network of gentile churches and the original home office (that continued to concentrate upon the Jewish market segment.) If the church was to avoid (1) being ripped apart by internal divisions and/or (2) being weakened by focusing upon only one target market, a rethinking of the relationship between the home office and the international division was essential.

The International Division Dominates

By the end of Paul and Barnabas' first missionary journey, a showdown between the Jewish oriented Christians of Jerusalem and Paul's network of churches, dominated by gentiles, was coming to a head. Paul had blatantly gone after the gentile market and was very successful in doing so. As a result, the Jewish wing of the church was losing power and rapidly becoming outnumbered. Just as in a modern proxy fight, the home office, knowing its dominance was being threatened, made overt efforts to disrupt the successes of its rivals.

Opposing this last ditch attempt of the home office to emphasize the Jewish heritage and make it a prerequisite for membership, Paul and Barnabas went to Jerusalem to settle the matter once and for all; the meeting that followed is called "The Council of Jerusalem." By this time, the power of the old guard was so undermined that Peter (fearful of the Judaizers on earlier occasions) stood squarely in Paul's camp, favoring an international strategy that generalized Christianity so all could embrace the church. Supporting Paul, Peter affirmed that his conversion of Cornelius was not a fluke or an isolated case and he rhetorically asked why the organization's international representatives were being asked to wear a "yoke" of specific ethnic traditions that would handicap their effectiveness (*Acts*, 15-9-1 1.)

While the Council of Jerusalem was conducted in a manner that allowed the old guard to save face, it established the dominance of the international division and its priorities. Acknowledging the legitimacy of Paul's sales methods, he was recognized as a legitimate member of the organization. A formal division of labor was set up; Peter, James, and John were authorized to continue converting Jews while Paul and Barnabas were instructed to direct their efforts towards the gentiles (*Galatians* 2.9.) This decision, in effect, transformed Paul from an international franchise holder to the CEO of the most powerful division of the organization. In the process, Paul gained political leverage, respect, and personal clout within the entire church while maintaining control over his original sphere of operations. He also maintained the autonomy of the international division. The old guard, in contrast, gave Paul (their chief rival) an important managerial slot in the organization and conceded that they would continue their work among the Jews, a segment of shrinking importance that was emerging as just another of many different target markets. This decision, therefore, simultaneously shifted power towards Paul and the international division and away from Jerusalem and the original home office.

At least in the short term, however, many gentile and Judaic Christians (both harboring specific and distinct ethnic traditions) would continue to live together and attend the same church; this created a source of potential friction. Although the Council agreed that gentiles could be saved without embracing Jewish traditions, internal disruption needed to be prevented. James, a strict Jew and brother of Jesus, forged a compromise, asking "that in Christian communities where Jewish and Gentile converts had to live together in harmony, the Gentiles should abstain from certain practices that were particularly offensive to the ingrained sensibilities of their Jewish brethren" (Castelot 1967 14.)

This proposal demonstrates a profound understanding of cultural relativity and the methods of trans-cultural interaction proposed by business-oriented anthropologists such as Edward T. Hall. Both James and Hall were aware that when different peoples live and work together, great care must be exercised to avoid unintentionally offending coworkers and clients. Both James and Hall also realized that seemingly innocent habits can disrupt, alienate, and bring havoc to an otherwise harmonious situation. Since many early churches were populated by more than one ethnic group, James' proposal was appropriate and similar suggestions are echoed even today by managerial experts such as Edward T. Hall.

After the Council of Jerusalem, the power of the old home office was clearly undermined and the Christian church became truly international. By offering more local autonomy than Mithraism, an international rival, ultimate success resulted. Paul (the best known example of an international marketing manager from ancient times) established an independent franchise system, used a localized marketing strategy to make it flourish, and he finally emerged as the dominant figure of the entire organization.

Ancient Analogies and the Modern World

If applying contemporary business concepts to earlier eras is not merely to be "new wine in old skins" the analysis must contribute to our knowledge, not just provide cute examples. Indeed, I picked up and put down the foregoing analysis on several occasions because I feared that it might shallowly apply modern concepts to an ancient and sacred example and, in the process, cheapen both. Today, I am firmly convinced that the *New Testament* really does provide a classic case of international marketing strategies in conflict and that it provides valuable clues to modern international management.

As the third millennium begins, striking parallels between the Roman Empire and today's world are increasingly apparent. Both eras saw the rise of impressive transportation and communications networks that were able to facilitate international contact in exciting ways. Both viewed profound economic growth as a direct result of these advances. In our time, participants in the international arena have constantly debated the pros and cons of localized versus standardized marketing strategies; in doing so, they parallel the ancients who faced similar situations.

In recent decades we have seen the buzzwords of "globalization" and the "republic of technology" (Levitt 1983) being bandied about. In essence, these concepts insist that modern culture is being profoundly homogenized and that those on the international scene should consciously strive to market products world-wide in similar and universal ways. Although Theodore Levitt and other contemporary globalizers are aware that such tactics cannot always be employed, homogenization and globalization often emerge as the yardsticks by international business practice is judged.

When looking at Roman-era, parallels, Paul emerges as the patron saint of localizers. Although simultaneously being challenged by two distinct rivals (the Jerusalem traditionalists and the followers of Mithra) he rose to the occasion and forged a path based on the distinctiveness of specific groups.

The traditionalists of the Jerusalem, Jewish-oriented church applied ethnocentric tactics in ways that duplicate the excesses, blunders, and "boners" that are fictionally recreated in the *Ugly American*, a blockbuster "docu-novel" about American foreign service in Southeast Asia during the Cold War (Lereder and Burdick 1958.) Both American diplomats and Jewishly-oriented Christians of Paul's day placed a profound emphasis upon the specific details of their cultures and they both lost international successes they could have won because of their ethnocentric blindness. Both groups only accepted clients who were willing to totally to embrace lifestyles that paralleled those of the home office. Closing my eyes, I can almost picture Louis Sears, the ineffectual American Ambassador, of *The Ugly American* among the traditionalists of the early Jerusalem church since both encouraged the "culture genocide" of their clients (i.e., the abandonment and demise of a society's cultural traditions) as a prerequisite for receiving benefits. Because Sears and the Jerusalem traditionalists chose this course of action, the efforts of both were ultimately doomed.

The followers of Mithras form a second set of globalizers that confronted Paul. They believed skilled management, organizational tightness, and experience-curve benefits would allow their organization to maintain a dominant position. Using a classic globalization strategy, the followers of Mithras possessed a highly skilled hierarchical management, they perfected their product, and they marketed their organization in similar ways throughout the known world. Their flaw lay in placing more emphasis on organizational and product uniformity than upon nesting the services rendered within the cultural milieu of each specific target market. In the final analysis, neither the Judiazers nor the cult of Mithras could outdistance the gains made by a skilled localizer who possessed a profound respect for the beliefs, attitudes, and lifestyles of other peoples. Paul was willing to adjust the services being offered so they would mesh with the preferences of specific target markets. Abandoning a "home office mentality", he overtly, concretely, and profoundly adjusted each local organization to reflect domestic conditions. Doing so, Paul changed the course of history.

Keeping parallels with the Roman Empire in mind, the effectiveness of Paul's locally centered marketing campaign points to the importance of dealing with people on their own terms and adjusting the products being offered them accordingly. Doing so is a legitimate alternative, not merely an after thought or "booby prize" to embrace when universal strategies don't work.

References

Castelot, J. J. (1967) "Judaizers", *New Catholic Encyopaedia* Vol. 8, New York, McGraw-Hill.)

Chiovaro. F F., (1967) "Presbyter" *New Catholic Encyclopedia*, Vol. 11, (New York McGraw Hill p. 745.

Duchense-Guillemin, J.(1967) , "Mithras and Mithraism", *New Catholic Encyclopedia* Vol 9 (New York: McGraw Hill) p.982.

Wicks, Robert R. (1957) "The Epistle of Philippans" *The Interpreter's Bible* Volume 11 (New York, Abingdon Press.)

Lederer, W. and Burdick, E (1958) *The Ugly American*, (New York: Norton.)

Levitt, Theodore (1960) "Marketing Myopia", *Harvard Business Review.*

Levitt, Theodore (1983) *The Marketing Imagination* (New York: The Free Press.)

Packer. J.. *et al* (1980) *The Bible Almanac*, (Nashville, Thomas Nelson.)

Schroedcr, F. J. (1967) "Paul" *New Catholic Encyclopedia* Vol. 11 (New York: Norton)

Showerman, G (1910) "Mithras", *Encyclopedia Britannica*, Vol. 18, pp. 622-4.

Chapter 2

The Positioning of Good News

The last chapter showed how a close reading of the *New Testament* reveals that early Christian leaders were consciously aware of various marketing tactics that are still employed today. These leaders, furthermore, argued among themselves regarding the specific strategies that should be used to most effectively mold their organization. Initially, a hierarchy centered in Jerusalem embraced what may be considered a narrow "niching" strategy designed to cater to the needs of a fairly circumscribed target market (the Jewish subculture.) The strategists who favored this option (the Judaisers) insisted that Christianity was merely a faction of Judaism, and, therefore, Christians were obliged to follow all Jewish laws including dietary customs and even circumcision. These Christians believed that non-Jews could be converted to the faith, but only if they adopted a wide range of uniquely Jewish customs.

The rivals of the Judaisers, in contrast, believed that requiring all converts to abandon their distinctive lifestyles and adopt the ways of an alien ethnic group (the Jews) would build resistance to the organization and the services it offered. St. Paul, an avowed missionary to the gentiles, was particularly outspoken in this regard and he insisted that the Jewish flavor of Christianity should be relaxed when serving gentile clients. Eventually the polemic between these rival factions reached a head, and proponents of each position met at a policy making session known as the "Council of Jerusalem." At that meeting, St. Paul and his allies won the day; Christianity ceased being a Jewish sect and it emerged as a flexible religion that could be incorporated into different cultures and lifestyles. This inclusive strategy increased the ability of early Christianity to market itself throughout the Roman world.

This debate within the early church is often paralleled by dissension that rack modern organizations as they seek to move into the international sphere. One group of strategists, the Judiazers, advocated selling the same product in a similar way over a wide area to many different target markets. Such "global" strategies may reap certain benefits, but they can also hinder attempts to cater to a plurality of markets in strategic ways. A more flexible marketing strategy, such as that advocated by Paul, adjusts the organization and its products to the situation at hand. This approach proved to be most effective and transformed Christianity into a world-wide religion.

A Tangled Situation

Looking at various books of the *New Testament* is useful because doing so demonstrates how their authors, consistent with St. Paul's emphasis, tailored their messages with specific people in mind. The ability to examine these tactics and how they were applied in the first century is made easier by the fact that the four gospels are all basic statements of Christianity that were written to influence distinct target markets. In other words, all the gospels promoted Christianity while each writer(s) phrased the message in ways designed to influence specific target markets. Taken as a collective whole, these documents form a multi-pronged marketing and public relations campaign of a not-for-profit organization.

This chapter deals with each Gospel as a specific example of marketing and promotional activities. What is said (and what is not said in specific texts) will be discussed in terms of the target market being addressed and with reference to the specific goals of the authors.

Mark: A Non-Strategic Chronicle

Mark is generally recognized as the first gospel to be written and, as such, it influenced the other three to various degrees. Enjoying the status of a primary source, it appears to be the least influenced by the concerns of advertising and public relations. *Mark* may have exerted less of a promotional thrust because it was addressed to those who already embraced Christianity. Marketers, however, are familiar with the term "internal marketing" that refers to promotions directed within the organization. Nonetheless, this type of advocacy is very different from marketing communications that are designed to win new customers. Thus "Mark's purpose was accordingly...intensely practical. He was writing a book for the guidance and support of his fellow Christians in a situation of intense crisis. The martyrdoms had fallen off but there was no assurance-with Nero on the throne-when they might begin again" (Luccock 1951 634.)

As Cereoke explains, Mark created little that was unique to him, satisfying himself with committing to paper what already existed-primarily in the oral tradition. Thus, "The purpose of Mark as a whole is clearly catechetical. The evangelist creates no new theology concerning Jesus' person and role, but places himself at the service of the existing faith of the church to give it firm foundation " (Ceroke 1967 233–40.)

Mark's gospel, therefore, seems to have recorded what already existed with a minimum of strategic alternations. What the evangelist does for the most part is to tell the story of Jesus' life as it was known and understood in Christian circles. Fact and theology had already been combined in this tradition and what is often described as Mark's theology is really the early Christian belief as to the historic facts." (Branscomb 1928 6.)

Although *Mark* has a weak marketing thrust because it was largely intended to codify preexisting beliefs, the writing style also prevented the document from being an excellent promotional document. Mark fell victim to one of the oldest traps to befall a copywriter: he forgot his true purpose. Biblical scholars observe that Mark began to tell his story for its own sake and the effectiveness of his work suffers as a result.

Marketing professionals have long realized that copywriters sometimes fail to communicate effectively because they ignore the true purpose of their work (influencing a target market) and strive, instead, to achieve some other goal, such as entertaining an audience or creating literary art. American television provides a number of such examples: a series of commercials for Wendy's hamburgers aired during the 1980s, for example, was amusing and spawned the popular phrase "where's the beef" which cropped up in the 1984 presidential campaign. The amusing nature of the commercials, however, backfired since it overshadowed and blunted Wendy's message. The campaign, therefore, largely failed as a marketing communication, even though it won high applause as entertainment.

Examples such as this are often used to warn copywriters to avoid communicating in ways that are so interesting or so funny that the audience is distracted from the specific ideas being conveyed. Mark's gospel appears to embody this flaw in copywriting technique; because Mark tried to tell a good story full of excitement and vivid characters, the message becomes diffused, blurred, and might not adequately influence the reader. Certainly, Mark provides interesting anecdotes and examples that other authors were able to rework in strategic ways. Nonetheless, *Mark* fails as an example of excellent marketing communications.

This shortcoming is probably due, in part, to the fact that Mark was a poor writer. He has a weak command of the written word and he overworked certain commonly used words and phrases: the sure sign of a novice. Today, the fact that his style is undistinguished and sometimes downright poor is masked by the tendency for translators to present his thoughts using better and more literate phraseology than Mark, himself, was able to provide.

Realizing that Mark had grave literary shortcomings, however, we find his inability to act as a skilled copywriter entirely plausible and predictable.

In summary, of all the four Gospels, *Mark* is least influenced by marketing strategies and the techniques of marketing communication. In part, this is due to the fact that the book was written for those who were already Christian; as a result, he may not have been overly concerned with winning new followers. In addition, Mark's poor writing skills and his attempt to make his gospel a "good story" undercut whatever attempts he might have made to create an excellent marketing-oriented document. Nonetheless, the book was a goldmine of examples and details that other authors used when writing their own gospels. In spite of (and possibly because of) Mark's naiveté as a writer, he infused his account with a richness of detail that gives the text a vividness lacking in the other three gospels. The fact that Mark apparently knew St. Peter personally and worked closely with him for a number of years also gives Mark's gospel a special significance. But as an example promotional literature it has grave shortcomings.

Matthew: A Targeted Gospel

In its earliest days, Christianity was considered to be a subset of Judaism. As a result, Christians were expected to behave according to Jewish laws and customs. When such requirements became a stumbling block to the efforts of missionaries, however, Paul relaxed this policy in order for the religion to better mesh with the lifestyles of the larger Hellenistic world. Such a strategic decision, however, did not prevent missionaries who worked among the Jews from presenting Christianity in ways that would uniquely appeal to members of this ethnic group. In order to cater to a Jewish audience, a Christian literature that forcefully responded to Hebrew culture, beliefs, and traditions was required. The *Gospel of Saint Matthew* is a specific example of promotional literature directed at this target market.

Matthew's conscious and deliberate catering to the Jewish community becomes obvious as soon as his rhetorical style is considered. Although all the gospels acknowledge that Jesus fulfilled *Old Testament* prophecies, Matthew dwells upon this theory and directly quotes the *Old Testament* more than *Mark* and *Luke*, the other two synoptic gospels, combined. As any good copywriter knows, a piece of promotional literature needs to address people on their own terms and that is exactly what Matthew did. By emphasizing that Christianity fulfilled Jewish prophecy and by constantly placing Christianity within the context of the *Old Testament*, Matthew readily accomplished this goal.

Besides merely quoting the *Old Testament* extensively, Matthew took certain liberties with the text in order to manipulate the available materials to better influence his Jewish audience. The most overt of these actions occurs when he actually invents a verse which reinforces a key part of his argument and attributes it to the prophets. Jesus resided in Nazareth and Matthew wished to show that the Jewish savior was preordained to come from that city. Quoting *Matthew* (2:23) we find "he went and in a town called Nazareth: that there might be fulfilled what was spoken through the prophets, 'He shall be called a Nazarene'.

According to J. P. Shelton, however: "This is not in the *Old Testament* nor is Nazareth ever mentioned there" (Shelton 1967.) Clearly, Matthew added a kind of "testimonial" attributed to the prophets (well respected "opinion leaders") in order to bolster his "sales pitch." Structurally, this is identical to the actions of a modern advertising agency that hires an admired spokesperson to mouth convincing advertising copy.

Although Matthew's inventing of a prophet's prediction is his most blatant manipulation, the example is hardly isolated. On numerous occasions, Matthew either quotes the *Old Testament* out of its proper context or combines different texts to create a composite statement that that creates a new and distinct meaning. Although many examples of copywriting sleight of hand exist in *Matthew*, I will remind the reader of just one well-known example of such tactics. *Matthew* (2:15) states: "Out of Egypt, I called my son." Matthew is quoting *Hosea* (11:1) in order to demonstrate that Jesus was preordained to live in Egypt for a period of time before moving to Palestine. Doing so bolsters the claim that Christ's life was divinely directed and was consistent with Jewish prophecy. Looking at the *Hosea* text in its proper context, however, it becomes obvious that the quotation refers to the exodus in which the Jewish people, as an entity, left Egypt hundreds of years previously and that the "he" in the quotation is a collective term refers to the Jewish people as a group.

Matthew was a skilled copywriter who crafted his message in ways that appealed to his Jews. Matthew, furthermore, knew how to use the statements of well respected opinion leaders to advantage. Indeed, Matthew's writing provides copious examples of how to market spiritual well being (an intangible product) to a circumscribed group that possesses its own special character and orientation.

Besides using a rhetorical style and a set of copywriting tactics designed to advance his sales pitch, Matthew chose to include materials which possessed uniquely persuasive powers among his Jewish audience. "The intention is to show abundantly how the life and death of Jesus Christ fit perfectly with the common heritage of all Jews, the *Old Testament* revelation" (Shelton 1967 500.)

Although Matthew relies heavily on *Mark,* for example, he begins his Gospel with a long and drawn-out genealogy (*Matthew* 1:1–17) having no precedent in *Mark.* The obvious purpose of this prologue is to demonstrate that Jesus was descended from David as predicted in the *Old Testament.* Not only does Matthew assert that Jesus was descended from David, he also artificially lumps Christ's ancestors into three groups of 14 generations each. This technique is used because the ancient Jews believed certain numbers were magical and/or indicated divine intervention. Indeed, Matthew actually forced this division on his materials (as indicated by various inaccuracies and gaps that exist in his reciting of the genealogy.)

To understand the degree to which Matthew was responding to the expectations of his Jewish target market, a comparison with another genealogy that appears in *Luke* is useful. Luke's genealogy is more accurate and is not artificially broken down into three sub-groups of 14 generations each. Most significantly, however, Luke's Christ is descended from Adam, (the father of all mankind) and not merely David, a major Jewish hero who was predicted to be the ancestor of the Savior. These differences clearly demonstrate that Matthew, unlike the authors of the other gospels, was carefully placing his message within Jewish traditions and that he overtly orchestrated his materials with this goal in mind.

While Matthew added material unique to his gospel in order to cater to a circumscribed target market, he also reworked the *Gospel of Mark* in order to better underscore his message. As argued earlier, although *Mark* provides good source material, he was a rather inept marketing communicator. Because of this weakness and because *Matthew* was targeted towards a specific subculture, Matthew often subtly changed Mark's text in ways that would more effectively influence Jewish readers.

The Baptism of Christ is a case in point. In *Mark,* when Christ is baptized, God addresses Christ as follows: "Thou art my beloved Son, in thee I am well pleased" (*Mark* 1:11.) Reading *Mark* one gets the impression that Jesus may have been unaware of his monumental role and that he needed to be informed of it. Such a reading raises a whole set of thorny questions and "red herrings" that the church would be better off avoiding. In general, such questions would ponder if Jesus was preordained to be the Son of God or if he was merely an especially pious man whom God saw and then accepted as his son. Any suggestion that God chose Jesus *ex post facto,* of course, would undercut both the virgin birth theory and the significance of Matthew's belabored genealogy, both of which imply a long and drawn-out plan on God's part.

In this situation, Matthew slightly altered *Mark* to read, (Matthew 3:17) "And behold, a voice from the heavens said, 'This is my beloved Son in whom

I am well pleased." Note that in Matthew's version, the difficult questions raised in Mark's original verse are eliminated. God merely tells the crowd that Christ is his son, and we can well imagine that Christ knew this all along. To bolster this doctrine, Matthew added a statement from John the Baptist, not in *Mark*, that indicates that John the Baptist was aware that Jesus was the Son of God even before the baptism took place. John says (Matthew 3:14) "It is I who ought to be baptized by thy and dost thou come to me?" Since this statement demonstrates John accepting a subservient position, it could be employed to counter any speculations that John the Baptist, not Jesus, was the savior.

Another example of Matthew giving a special Jewish flavor to what he borrowed from *Mark* involves an episode where the Apostles were without food on Sabbath and they gather some grain to eat. Pointing to that event, the Pharisees chide (*Mark* 2:24) "Why are they doing what is not lawful [working] on the Sabbath? " In the exchange which follows, Mark's Christ affirms that it is legitimate for hungry men to feed themselves; he states: "The Sabbath was made for man and not man for the Sabbath" (*Mark* 2:28.) The basic idea conveyed by Mark is that the established religious leaders had become so involved with ritual and in outward signs of piousness that they were unable to take legitimate human needs into account. *Matthew* (12: 5–6), in contrast, adds to Jesus' comment: "Have you not read in the law, that on the Sabbath day the priests in the temple break Sabbath and are guiltless? But I tell you that one greater than the temple is here." Such an addition firmly asserts that Jesus is greater than the Temple and his presence, not hunger, makes the apostles' behavior legitimate. It also portrays the apostles as religious leaders who, because of their privileged status, can overlook some minor requirements of Jewish protocol. Mark's story, which merely points to the reactionary behavior of certain establishment types in a time of change, is transformed by Matthew into a strong statement that Christ, being the Son of God, can suspend or change Jewish traditions at will. Such sentiments, of course, were at the heart of Matthew's message, and he frequently wove such ideas into material that had been borrowed from *Mark*.

Such examples, and the many others that they represent, demonstrate how Matthew edited and reworked his source material so that it would more effectively influence his specific target market. As has been emphasized, Matthew sought to overtly cater to the Jewish subculture, and, for that reason, it is an ancient example of copywriting that was aimed at a specific market segment.

John: A More Universal Gospel

The Gospel of St. John is a difficult book to understand for a number of reasons. First, it appears to be the last gospel to be written and, as such, was the furthest removed from the actual life of Christ. As form criticism tells us, the process of oral transmission may have taken its toll and blurred or transformed some details. Secondly, while the other gospels follow a similar, synoptic pattern, *John* cannot be harmonized with them even though the author obviously incorporates many of the events they chronicle into his gospel. Thirdly, and possibly most importantly, the author(s) of *John* was obviously a brilliant and original thinker, not merely a passive reporter of the available facts, or even a fine tuner intent upon retelling *The Gospel* of Mark to a specific group of people, as *Matthew* had done. Although indebted to the preexisting traditions regarding Christ, the vision of Christian doctrine in *John* has little precedent and, therefore, it demands a careful and thoughtful examination.

Many earlier scholars argued simply (or simplistically) that *John* was written to supplement the synoptic gospels, not replace them. By the time *John* was written, the other gospels had become available and yet another retelling of the events of Christ's life was not needed. Earlier scholars reasoned that, as a result, John chose to provide a new perspective and not duplicate or edit what was already available (Walsh 1977.)

In the nineteenth century, this theory survived and it was refined to state that John's purpose was to convey a broader and more complete picture of Jesus. This made *John* appear to be a sort of appendix that painted an in-depth portrait of Christ, the man: a much-needed portrayal unavailable elsewhere.

Many twentieth century scholars, in contrast, have come to believe that *John* was written to replace, not to augment, the earlier gospels. According to that hypothesis, John sensed that the era in which he lived was very different from that in which the synoptic gospels had been written; changing times created the need for a gospel that was tailored for the new age. The pioneer of this school of thought, Rudolph. Bultmann (1971) argues that a close reading reveals that the doctrines of *John* are strongly connected with Hellenistic thought and orientations. Such interpretations, of course, were further developed by B. W. Bacon in his *The Gospel of the Hellenists* (1933) and in many other places.

These reflections regarding the overt purpose of *John* demonstrate that John was creating a universal promotional literature for the church to which the gentile Hellenistic world could respond.

The entire ancient world of John's era was strongly influenced by Hellenistic culture. Although the Romans ruled politically, the cultural life of educated people throughout the empire was Greek. Because Hellenistic thought was a sort of intellectual "lingua franca" for the educated opinion leaders of the times, a gospel that discussed Christ in Hellenistic terms would constitute a promotional document of almost universal application. *John* is that global document.

The doctrine that Christ was the only son of God and that salvation comes from him dominates the *Gospel of John.* Indeed, better than any other gospel author, John subordinated his subject matter to the specific message he is advancing. The other gospels, in contrast, often become entangled with various side issues that are of only marginal significance to Christian doctrine. As we have seen, for example, Mark strove to write a "good story" for its own sake and, as a result, his efforts are compromised as marketing communications. Although both *Matthew* and *Luke* are more focused and constrained, they also lack the singleness of purpose that is the hallmark of good promotional literature. Specifically, *Matthew* and *Luke* depict Christ as a compassionate man who performs miracles because he is sorry for the people he meets. Although it is, perhaps, worthwhile to know Christ was a "nice man", simply dwelling on Christ's kindness draws the reader's attention away from important aspects of doctrine that need to be emphasized.

John's handling of Christ's miracles, in contrast, is typically guided by his desire to show that Jesus was the son of God and that salvation comes through him. Thus, when a friend of Christ dies, John's Christ observes this event can be used "for the glory of God, that through it the Son of God may be glorified" (11:4.) While the various miracles in the Synoptic Gospels are ends in themselves, even when they benefit total strangers, John's Christ is so calculating that he is strategic even when restoring a personal friend from the dead. Thus, before raising Lazarus, *John*'s Christ cannot resist making a speech which underscores the doctrine which *John* is presenting (*John* 1: 25-6): "I am the resurrection and the life; he who believes in me, even if he should die, shall live; and whosoever lives and believes in me shall never die."

The *Gospel of John,* therefore, is a carefully constructed document that deals with the universal theme of salvation for all people. The author(s) of *John* self-consciously orchestrates the events he chronicles in order to advance his specific goal. And since the author(s) subordinates the material he uses in order to advance his specific sales pitch, *John* is an excellent example of the copywriter's art.

Besides being a model of excellent copywriting, *John* also reflects the desire to create a universal marketing communication, not a circumscribed document of limited application. The message is phrased in universal ways to which all Hellenistic intellectuals could respond and it provided a sales pitch that was geared towards the educated and affluent opinion leaders of his era.

Luke: The Public Relations Specialist

Different in many important respects, the Gospels of *Mark, Matthew,* and *John* were all written for clients (or potential clients) of the organization and they can be viewed as marketing communications directed at the consumer. The efforts of these three gospels, of course, represent but one kind of communication used to advance the goals of an organization. Organizations also need to build a good image among the general public and with governmental officials. By doing so, organizations can minimize opposition and win friends.

Consider the tobacco industry. Where and when legally permitted, it pursues massive advertising campaigns directed at the ultimate consumer. In addition, it engages in activities that are not specifically designed to win customers per se, but, instead, are intended to create a good image. Thus, the industry actively engages in public relations and pursues what in the United States is called "lobbying": providing governmental officials with information that is designed to make them more sympathetic to the industry and the specific firms that comprise it.

A long respected theory states that the *Gospel of Luke* and *Acts* were addressed to members of the Roman civil service. An alternative explanation is that Luke was addressing Christians in order to provide them with advice regarding how to present the faith to the larger Roman world. Thus, Brown observes (1997 271-2) "A more plausible suggestion is that the Lucan writing could help the Christian readers/hearers...to know that there was nothing subversive in their origins, nothing that cause them to be in conflict with Roman governance, and that it was false to assimilate Jesus and his immediate followers to the Jewish revolutionaries who had embroiled the Roman armies in war in the late 60s."

In both theories, however, the end result is the same: Roman officials would be told that the church was no threat to Rome. The only difference is that in one case the information goes straight from Luke to the Roman officials and in the other case, it passes through an intermediate source: Luke's readers.

Accepting such a perspective, *Luke* is best viewed as a public relations document that was created for lobbying purposes among the Roman civil service. Internal evidence suggests that *Luke* was specifically written for a specific Roman official named Theophilus and the author consciously hoped that by presenting a positive overview of the church to this influential leader more favorable treatment might result.

Like any skilled public relations practitioner, Luke strove to make his lobbying efforts seem objective and straightforward. He states: "Inasmuch as many have undertaken to draw up a narrative concerning...[the church] I also have determined, after following up all things carefully from the very first, to write for thee an orderly account that thou may understand." (*Luke* 1:1–4)

Significantly, *Luke* mentions a number of other accounts of the church which Theophilus might have read; perhaps these were negative in tone: an attack on the church that Luke needed to counter. This, of course, is typical work for a lobbyist or public relations specialist and *Luke*, while providing an "orderly account" also portrays the church in a light that was designed to positively influence the Roman government. First, and most importantly, Luke sought to emphasize that Christianity was not subversive and was not a threat to the Roman Empire.

The first century of the Christian church was an era when the Roman establishment looked with suspicion upon alien religions (and put tight restrictions on some, such as the cult of Bacchus.) Although the Roman government recognized religions that were friendly to the empire and presented no threat, others were suppressed. Indeed, under the reign of Nero Christians had been accused of burning the city of Rome and, as a result, many Christians had been tortured and killed. Luke wrote during a lull in such suppression and, understandably, he wished to seize the moment and dispel any suspicion that Christianity was anti-Roman.

For this reason, *Luke* and *The Acts of the Apostles* (originally written as volume two of *Luke*) dealt with the Roman government in a most cordial manner. Luke belabors the point that Pontius Pilate, the Roman administrator involved in Christ's execution, was not responsible for the verdict and that Pilate actually tried to intercede on Christ's behalf. Pilate's wife, furthermore, refers to Christ as a "just man", and Luke's Pilate attempts to facilitate the release of Christ on numerous occasions. Such content is vital to Luke's message, since he wished to show that Christians did not hold a grudge against Rome for the death of Christ.

All the gospels acknowledge that the Jews (more specifically the Pharisees) were behind Jesus' execution, but *Luke* is more forceful in this regard. Luke's Pilate even refuses to co-operate with a Jewish scheme to prevent Christ's followers from gaining access to his body after the execution. Roman authorities, therefore, are depicted as acting in a reasonable, compassionate, and professional manner. According to the picture painted by *Luke*, the death of Christ cannot be blamed on Roman injustice, and Rome, therefore, should not be fearful of Christian reprisals.

Besides quashing fears that Christianity might be anti-Roman, Luke also found it useful to suggest that Christianity was in no way a threat to Mithraism, a religion that was popular among Roman officials. As we saw in the last chapter, Mithraism was a cult patronized by members of the Roman Army; since many retired military officers became important public officials, the Roman bureaucracy was undoubtedly predisposed towards that religion (See Chapter 2.) Even if Christianity was not a threat to Rome *per se*, pro-Mithras Roman officials might be hostile to the Church if they felt it rivaled or jeopardized their own faith. For Luke's gospel to be effective, he had to minimize this possible conflict of interest. By dismissing the possible rivalry between Mithraism and Christianity, Luke seems to have emphasized that his organization did not actively seek to serve a target market that was valued by a powerful and established rival. *Luke*'s emphasis upon the role of women in Christianity could have been one way of doing so. Great attention, for example, is given to Jesus' relationships with women and to the important role of various female members of the church. This emphasis upon women would have reassured devotees of Mithraism, since that religion was male-oriented. By emphasizing the role of females within the church, Luke presented a subtle argument that Christianity was not in direct competition with Mithraism and did not seek to serve the same target market.

Besides dismissing fears that Christianity might constitute a challenge that undercut the faith of many important Roman officials, *Luke* also emphasizes that numerous Romans had become Christian. St. Paul, for example, was actually a Roman citizen, a point emphasized by Luke throughout *Acts*. Luke, furthermore, discusses how other Romans were converted to Christianity. Thus, a Roman officer stationed at the cross becomes convinced that Jesus was the son of God. In this regard, Luke alters the wording of *Mark*, where the officer had merely observed that Christ was innocent. In this strategic retelling, a Roman soldier (the kind of witness whose opinion could influence members of the Roman civil service) affirms Jesus' divine status.

Luke, furthermore, tells us that the first non-Jew to become a Christian was an important Roman official. The commander of the Roman garrison at Jerusalem twice saved St. Paul from Jewish mobs. In *Acts*, Luke even tells us that St. Paul's jailer and his wife are converted to Christianity.

Such examples, which could easily be multiplied by a more in-depth analysis of Luke's writing, indicate that being Roman and being Christian were not mutually exclusive. Indeed, Luke overtly underscores that many respected Romans had already joined the church and that being Christian did undercut their disloyalty to Rome.

In summary, Luke was a lobbyist and a public relations specialist who strove to create a positive image for his organization: early Christianity. Doing so was intended to help soften Roman suppression and create an environment where the church could grow. *Luke* systematically presents the church as neither a threat to Rome nor to Mithraism, the faith of many powerful civil servants. Luke also pointed to the fact that Roman officials who had joined or supported the church had not lost their patriotism. Although there was currently a lull in the persecution of the church, Luke obviously felt the need to forcefully present the church in the best possible light in order to help forestall future persecution. Given this environment, Luke's work emerges as a textbook example of excellent public relations.

Unified, Multi-Pronged Communications

The four gospels of the *New Testament* can best be viewed as promotional literature; various theories and methodologies of marketing, therefore, are useful when interpreting these writings and when assessing the degree to which they were effective. *Mark* represents the kind of document which is often created by people who are not skilled in marketing communications. Even though the authors of such efforts might be highly informed and although such work might constitute a wealth of examples, they are not adequately focused and strategically oriented. *Mark*, however, has certain redeeming features; it is a well informed account, and since it was not written for specific promotional purposes, it possesses a wide range of detail and a variety of information which could later be used by other more promotionally oriented writers.

While *Mark* provided good raw materials, the authors of the other Gospels wrote with specific goals consciously in mind. *Matthew* sought to promote his organization to a circumscribed target market, the Jews. John, in contrast, forged a document of global application that would appeal to the larger Hellenistic world of Greece and Rome. Even 2,000 years later, marketers and advertising professionals continue to debate the pros and cons of these two strategies. In his classic article, "A Tiger in Every Tank?", for example, John Ryans (1969) discusses the fact that although advertising professionals often attempt to create a universal or global message doing so can be difficult or impossible to accomplish. All too often, Ryans suggests (Personal communication), strategists and copywriters must abandon global orientations to create a sales pitch which uniquely responds to a specific culture.

On many occasions when a global strategy is employed, the campaign does not attempt to market to the whole world and, instead, caters to a homogeneous subset of people spread out over a wide area. Thus, marketers who sell status goods may choose to market to well-to-do people throughout world (be they in the United States, England, or El Salvador.) These global strategies are really niching tactics which attempt to cater to a minority that shares some common trait (in this case wealth and status.) By doing so, respected and powerful opinion leaders are addressed.

John used such a strategy. In the Roman world, all educated people embraced Hellenistic perspectives. By presenting his message in Hellenistic terms, *John* speaks in convincing ways to the educated minority who lived throughout the Roman Empire. The fact that the author(s) of *John* wrote in a way that catered to educated and influential people complemented the more niched efforts of authors such as Matthew.

Although *Matthew, Mark,* and *John* were written to appeal to the consumer, this is but one type of organizational communication used to advance the goals of an organization. Public relations, that strives to create a positive environment in which organization exist, is significant even if it cannot be explicitly related to sales. Luke's work is clearly in the realm of public relations and it was consciously dedicated to building a good image for his organization among Roman officials. The *Gospel of Luke* reminds us that marketing strategies do not exist in a vacuum, and good public relations often supplements promotional campaigns directed towards customers and potential customers.

In the final analysis, the four gospels of the *New Testament* are examples of a promotional literature written 2,000 years ago. So viewed, we see that little has changed in the basic techniques and strategies that are employed. Interpreting the gospels with reference to modern marketing, advertising, and public relations methods, they and their goals can be better understood. In this way, they can provide illuminating examples to business methods and how they operated and functioned in ancient times.

References

Bacon, B.. W., *The Gospel of the Hellenists* (1933) (New York: Holt.)

Branscomb, B. H (1928.) *The Gospel of Mark* (New York.)Bultman, R., *The Gospel of John,* (1971) (Philadelphia: Westminster.)

Ceroke, C. P (1967) "The Gospel According to Mark", *New Catholic Encyclopedia* , Vol. 9, (New York: McGraw Hill) pp. 233–40)

Johnson, Sherman, E. "Matthew" (1951) *Interpreters Bible* Volume 7 (New York Abingdon Cokesbury Press) p. 231–50.

Luccock, Halford E. (1951) "Mark", in *The Interpreter's Bible* (New York: Abingdon-Cokesbury Press) p 629–48. 5.

Ryans, John, "A Tiger In Every Tank" (1969) Columbia *Journal of World Business* .

Shelton, J.P., "Gospel According to Matthew", *New Catholic Encyclopedia*, Vol. 9. New York: McGraw Hill, 1967, pp. 493–502.

Walle, Alf H. "Localized Strategies and the *Bible* of International Business", *European Journal of Marketing*, Vol. 21 #1, 1987, pp. 26–36.

Walsh, H. H. (1977) "Christianity" in *A Reader's Guide to the Great Religions* (New York: Free Press.)

Discussion of Part 1

Strange Bedfellows

Churches increasingly apply the tools and methods of business in order to be more effective. In doing so, pastors often envision that they are embracing ideas that were developed elsewhere. The business disciplines, in tandem with such perspectives, state that although they initially evolved within the private, profit-making sector, they have developed universal tools can benefit all organizations. Today, any number of books on church leadership use terms like the "marketing concept", "target market", "niching strategy", etc. as they attempt to introduce concepts beyond their original frame of reference: the free-enterprise system.

Chapters 1 and 2, in contrast, suggest that the bedrock concepts that modern business theorists and consultants celebrate as their inventions actually have a long history going back to ancient times. Indeed, a careful reading of the *New Testament* demonstrates that sophisticated marketing techniques were employed by the apostles and by those who wrote the gospels and the epistles.

Pointing out this reality has a number of relevant implications. First, when churches embrace marketing theory and practice, they are responding in a manner that reflects the work of the early church. Secondly, modern business theory is built, at least in part, upon this Biblical heritage. The implications of both of these observations resonate throughout this book.

This situation at first appears to be an example of "strange bedfellows", but is actually a classic case of "cross-disciplinary fertilization." And the benefits of "hybrid vigor" result.

Part 2

The Early Church and Ancient Spiritual Life

Prologue to Part 2

The Early Church and Ancient Spiritual Life

When the Christian church expanded beyond Palestine, it emerged as an interloper within a complex and well developed system of diverse religious and spiritual alternatives. While Biblical scholars perceive the distinctiveness of Christianity, those who sought spiritual comfort and eternal life during the early years of the church would have viewed it as just another of the mystery religions or philosophies that offered personal solace and/or salvation. The official religions of the Empire were almost entirely patriotic and collective in tone; as a result, they did little to comfort the individual. The mystery religions filled that void in ways that somewhat and superficially parallel what the church offered (i.e. companionship, the promise of eternal life, etc.) As a result of these inadvertent parallels, the average Greek or Roman would have viewed Christianity as just another of many alternatives.

This cluster of chapters looks at early Christianity as least as much from pagan eyes as from the perspective of believers. Although not inspired by or derived from the "History of Religions" school of the early 20th century (Hermann Gunkel, Johannes Weiss, Wilhelm Bousset, etc.), this work shares some similarities with that intellectual tradition. These essays, for example, seek to understand the relationship of early Christianity with other faiths such as (1) the mystery religion and (2) philosophies, such as stoicism and Epicureanism, which functioned as religions. In a manner that is reminiscent of the history of religions school, an apologetic tone towards the Christian faith is replaced by a more "objective" analysis that is focused upon (1) the religious environment into which the church was thrust and (2) how this milieu impacted the way that both insiders and outsiders viewed early Christianity. If the parts of the *New Testament* discussed in these chapters are read from this perspective, the reader can gain fruitful and robust perspectives regarding what was being said and the issues that were being confronted.

In the 1930s, the history of religion school faded because Biblical scholars felt that that a more pointed theological approach with a greater focus upon Christianity was more useful and appropriate. As a result, attention was directed increasingly inward and researchers became more prone to talk to themselves, not to outsiders. When this happened, vital inter-disciplinary linkages were weakened or broken. For better and/or for worse, during this period Biblical scholarship became more isolated and self-contained.

In general, this book suggests that Biblical scholarship will benefit from becoming more involved with other disciplines, seeking common ground, and working within a broader and more fluid intellectual context. These chapters suggest that by viewing the mystery religions and the philosophies of the ancient world as viable competitors that preceded Christianity (and long provided) alternatives to it), a better understanding of the *New Testament* results. Ultimately, seeking to understand how Christianity responded to its rivals has a significant theological purpose because doing so spotlights the challenges faced by the early church, as well as the strategies it used to assert itself. By viewing the rivals to the church on their own terms, Biblical scholarship can better understand how and why Christianity responded in the way that it did.

There is nothing new in this orientation. The emphasis here, however, is more skewed towards a pagan perspective than is usually found in contemporary Biblical scholarship. Thus, although the tact in these essays is not unique, the emphasis is more focused on pagan religions and Hellenistic philosophies than is often the case. When such perspectives are embraced, new and useful interpretations present themselves.

Today, many Biblical scholars prefer riveting most of their attention upon the challenges to Christianity that derived from the Jews and, perhaps, the Gnostics. Here, in contrast, I envision various mystery religions and philosophies as rivals competing for the loyalty of the people in the Hellenistic world. I see believers joining the church from within the context of the mystery religion system and initially assuming that Christianity was a typical component of it. I picture devotees of various cults attempting to merge Jesus with their gods, only to be rebutted in epistles that emphasize the distinctiveness of the savior and the religion he founded.

Within a few hundred years, the debates and the rivalries documented in these early writings died down and were largely forgotten. In this new environment, people found it hard to pinpoint the specifics of this great struggle. As a result, rhetoric aimed at specific rivals came to be interpreted as generic calls to avoid false teachers. That tradition of interpretation continues to this day.

But I sense that in the spiritual battleground of the early church, writers did not talk in glittering generalities. They had more important work to do and they faced specific battles that had to be fought. Those who crafted the gospels and epistles confronted real threats, challenges, and problems that derived from the pagan, Hellenistic world, not merely from Palestine and the Jews. By focusing more upon the context of these confrontations, teasing out the issues that were being discussed and positions that were being defended becomes possible. In this section, three examples of such analysis are provided.

In all four gospels, Roman soldiers gamble for Jesus' clothes at the foot of the cross. *John* is distinct, however, because the scene is shared by a microcosm of the early church. Contemporary Biblical scholars, not sensing any specific purpose for this alteration of the synoptic tradition tend to write off *John*'s editing as inadvertent. The author(s) of *John*, however, was a strategic writer who tended to alter the material used to better advance his theological agenda. If the changes in the gambling soldiers incident had no purpose, the author(s) was certainly acting out of context on this particular occasion.

Chapter 3, "The Three Marys and Mithras" argues that the *John*'s portrayal of the gambling soldiers created the opportunity to provide a commentary regarding Mithraism, a rival religion that was feared by the early church. Through a careful editing, the author(s) of *John* made a pointed analysis of Mithrasim that, while unrecognized by modern Biblical scholars, would have been obvious to a Hellenistic audience.

The parables are, of course, a major source of information about Jesus and how he felt about the world and the kingdom of God. Indeed, the Jesus Seminar tends to view the accounts of the parables as, perhaps, the most authentic records of what Jesus actually said and did. Nonetheless, the writers who incorporated the parables into the gospels may have (in a redactionary sort of way) tailored the accounts in tandem with theological positions they wished to advance. In Chapter 4, *Luke*'s parable of the "Rich Fool" is discussed from this perspective by arguing that it is a polemical and pejorative attack upon Epicurean philosophy. By comparing *Luke*'s version with a parallel version that appears within the *Gospel of Thomas*, it can be shown that the author of *Luke* took a generic parable about stewardship and greed and transformed it into a hostile and pointed attack upon a serious rival. *Luke*, furthermore, was written in order to (either directly or indirectly) encourage the Roman civil service to treat the church in a less hostile manner. Since the Roman civil service was dominated by stoic philosophy, a rival of the Epicureans, Luke's jab would have made a favorable impression upon those he sought to influence. A careful reading of *Luke*'s version of the parable and its context leads to the theory that the author of *Luke* may well have crafted his account accordingly. Thus, *Luke* was written with rival Hellenistic philosophies in mind; *Luke*'s reworking of the parable of the "Rich Fool" is an artifact of doing so.

The *Epistle of Jude* has been described as the most ignored book in the New Testament. Today, it tends to be dismissed (along with the other "catholic letters" as a generic call to avoid false teachers. Detractors, in addition, further discredit *Jude* by pointing to what is viewed as an overly heavy handed use of apocalyptic symbolism. As a result, many important scholars conclude that it has little theological value.

Chapter 5 "Christianity, Bacchus, and Sexual License" challenges this depiction. Far from being a pedestrian and generic letter, *Jude* was pointedly written to meet a specific challenge facing the early church: the tendency for members of the mystery religion system to incorporate Christianity in ways that could have resulted in the church abandoning it mission and losing its identity.

In specific, the author of *Jude* was concerned because advocates of the cult of Bacchus wanted to merge with Christianity and rework the church for its own purposes. Unnoticed by modern scholars, the counter attack presented in *Jude* resonates from specific references/analogies to the cult of Bacchus. Once these clues are interpreted, the epistle emerges as significant a profound defense of a church that was threatened with the possibility of being swallowed up and reformulated by the Hellenistic mystery religion system it wanted to transcend.

Collectively, these three essays demonstrate that Biblical scholarship can be invigorated in positive and productive ways by becoming more fully intertwined with classical studies and the history of the Hellenistic mystery religions. While the decline of the history of religion school in the 1930s may be justified, it appears that Biblical scholarship "threw the baby out with the bathwater" in the process. Much can be gained by nesting the early Christian experience within the Hellenistic world. In order to understand the richness of the gospels and epistles, such an understanding is necessary. While Biblical scholars accept this premise, they may need to act more aggressively in that regard.

Chapter 3

The Three Marys and Mithra:

A Difference of Little Consequence?

In all four gospels, there exists an account of Roman soldiers gambling around the cross, hoping to win Jesus' clothes. In *Matthew* (27:54), (15:39), and *Luke* (23:34), this anecdote is freestanding (aside from it being nested within the larger event of the crucifixion.) In the *Gospel of, John*, in contrast, the gambling soldiers are more fully discussed and they appear to be juxtaposed with loyal, grieving, and obedient believers. As usual, the account provided in the *Gospel of John* is distinctive when compared to the unity of the synoptic gospels.

There has been a tendency within *Biblical* criticism to suggest that this particular deviation in *John* was not motivated by any particular strategic purpose. Thus, the *New Interpreters Bible* observes:

> The episode [gambling of the soldiers] seems to have no distinctive theological significance for the forth Evangelist other than what it had for all of the evangelists (1995:31.)

Nonetheless, Biblical critics recognize that John deliberately crafts many alterations from the synoptic record in order to advance specific theological positions. Thus, if the changes regarding the soldiers at the cross are the fruit of casual and non-tactical editing, this was out of character for a writer who is known as thoughtful and strategic copyediting. Thus, even though Biblical scholars have discovered no reason for the distinctiveness of the gambling soldiers incident, as it appears in the *Gospel of John*, these changes may have been made to achieve some conscious goal.

This paper rethinks *John*'s unique treatment of the gambling soldiers incident by suggesting that the reworking is consistent with the goal of juxtaposing Christianity with Mithraism, a powerful rival religion that was popular among Roman soldiers when *John* was written. Such an argument presents a plausible and significant theological reason for the author(s) of *John* to have significantly edited the gambling soldiers incident.

In arguing this case, I will first discuss Mithrasim, its popularity among soldiers, and the fact that the cult was recognized as a rival to Christianity in the 1st century when *John* was written and first circulated. Having demonstrated the perceived challenge to Christianity presented by Mithrasim, a discussion of the distinctiveness of Christianity is provided. Building upon this background, the portrayal of the gambling soldiers (as it appears in *John*) is interpreted as a strategic theologically motivated juxtaposition of Mithraism and Christianity. The absence of the sympathetic Centurion (Roman army officer) at the cross in the *Gospel of John* eliminates a soldier (a probable devote of Mithras) who acts contrary to this portrayal. The argument concludes with a summary of the evidence, pointing out that the available facts consistently point to this theory and never contradict the argument that is presented.

Mithraism in the Roman Empire

Roman society in the 1st century AD was a fertile breeding ground for a wide variety of what have come to be called "mystery religions". As many scholars have argued, the "official" state religions, as they evolved in the Roman world, had come to reinforce and serve the needs of the government and society at large. Thus, Sir James Frazer observes:

> Greek and Roman society was built on the conception of the subordination
> of the individual to the community of the citizens to the state; it set the safety
> of the commonwealth as the supreme aim of conduct (Frazer 1935 300.)

As Merkeyback (1994) continues: "One of the most profound reasons for the success of the mystery religions must have been the majority of inhabitants of the Roman Empire had no opportunity of participating in the government of the state or exercising any influence on it, as had been possible in the …[Greek city states]. Consequently, everybody's energy was directed towards an individual striving. "

In addition, the circumscribed city-states that once provided people with a sense of identity and destiny had been replaced by a sprawling and impersonal empire. Hellenistic scholarship widely accepts the theory that this situation left the population alienated and unfulfilled. As a result, individual people found themselves emotionally cut adrift.

The emotional voids that resulted from this unenviable situation triggered a longing for people to join with something that was bigger than they were, on the one hand, but intimate enough to provide comfort and camaraderie, on the other. For some people (most typically, the educated minority) the solution to this situation lay in embracing formal philosophies, such as Stoicism and Epicureanism , which took on the character of religious entities., In this role, "Epicureans and Stoics alike addressed themselves to the task of redressing the imbalance between little man and huge world, of restoring dignity "...(Hadas 1961 vii.)

The emotional and spiritual needs of other segments of society tended to be satisfied by various mystery religions. Thus, while the state religions urged people to embrace society as a collective entity, "All this changed with the spread of... [the mystery religions] which inculcated the communion of the soul with God and its eternal salvation as the only objects worth living for." (Frazer 1935 300.)

The catalyst for the rise of the mystery religions is generally believed to have been the campaigns of Alexander the Great because his conquests triggered the processes that broke down the role of the city-state system and created an emotional void where people and their needs became isolated in a large and increasingly impersonal cultural and economic milieu. "[Due to Alexander the Great,] geographical and political horizons were enormously expanded, the insulation of the small city state was stripped away, and individuals had to come to terms with and find a place in the enormously enlarged environment." (Hadas 1961 vii.)

The improved lines of communication that were established within the Hellenistic world, furthermore, facilitated the introduction of a wide variety of foreign belief structures that could be transformed into mystery religions. As a result, many religious ideas were imported from the East, including the god Mithras.

The resulting environment provided people with new spiritual opportunities that came to play an important function in their lives. Serving this much needed role, these religions thrived. The mystery religion movement had begun to mature by the first century AD and it gave rise to a dizzying array of cults that promised personal salvation of one kind or another. In this atmosphere, both Roman Mithraism and Christianity grew to prominence.

One theory asserts that the Mithraism of the Roman world was an imported Persian religion. That is the basic thesis of *The Mysteries of Mithra* (1956) by Franz Cumont (a pioneering Mithra specialist.) Modern scholarship, in contrast, suggests that Roman Mithraism may have been a distinct religion, although based, somewhat, on Persian precedents (Hinnells 1975 xiii.)

As Monigliano has observed, "late in the first century Mithraism began to spread through the Roman empire" (1987 188.) It was one the last mystery religions to take hold in the Roman world (Gordon 1972 95) and it can be viewed as a classic example of the human striving for a more fulfilling and satisfying religious life that was centered upon the emotional needs of believers and their personal feelings. In the case of Mithraism, "The cult appealed to the Roman world because of its mysteriosophic views which centered on the concept of the life of the soul and its ascension through the seven planetary spheres. The ascension was symbolized by the seven grades of initiation , culminating in the transcendent level of fixed stars" (Gnoli 1987.)

The mood of the Mithratic religion is somewhat reflected in Rudyard Kipling's poem "A Song to Mithras" (which he indicates in a subtitle is the "Hymn of the XXX Legion: circa AD 350".) The poem reads in part, "Mithras, also a soldier, give us strength for the day....Mithras, also a soldier, teach us to die aright" (Kipling 1990 426–27.)

As Gordon (1972 104) has pointed out, although most of the mystery religions provide a refuge from the cultural milieu in which people lived:

> The symbolic or 'cultural' and social structures of Mithraism replicate the basic symbolic and social structures [in which Mithratic devotes interacted]...particularly the army, and that the type of social experiences constructed by Mithraists by the order of god is the replica of their 'ordinary' social experience, but without the irrationalities and contradictions of that experience.

Thus, it was a religion ideally suited for military life.

Mithraism arose out of religious precedents that had their origins in Persia. The God Mithras was envisioned as the Sun God and portrayed as a soldier.

Mithra is essentially a deity of light; he draws the sun with rapid horses; he is the first to reach the summit of Mount Hara at the center of the earth , and from there watches...[over the Aryans]; he shines with his own light and in the morning the many forms of the world visible...Mithra has a clear significance as a warrior god (Gnolia 1987 579)

In addition, over time Mithras became associated with other Gods:

> It is well known that the cult of Mithras assimilated a large number of [Roman Gods. It was]...quite frequently associated with the gods of Apollo and Mercury...It seems evident, however, that Mithras was also conflate with the Celtic divinities and became well established in some of the old sanctuaries of Gallic Origin (Walters 1974 49)

Mithras was a Sun God and:

> No other focus of religion could have served so well to unite [diverse Gods] under a single image...Mithras was the sun or his agent...[one single inscription unites] Zeus, Helios, Sarapis and Mithras (McMullen 1969 68)

Mithra, being the Sun God could be connected with many different Pagan religions (which worshiped the sun as a male god who fertilies the female "earth mother" with its light and warmth.)

As is the case in any number of nature-based religions, the god of the sun tends to be identified with the cycles of life, death, and rebirth. As such, Mithra was believed to rise in the morning, live through the day (traveling across the sky), die at twilight, and return to life at dawn in an endless cycle of birth, service, death, and resurrection. For obvious reasons, the example of the resurrection of Mithra coupled with the promise that loyal believers could enjoy the same destiny of resurrection, made the religion especially popular among members of the military (who identified with Mithra as a fellow soldier) because they were often called upon to risk their lives in battle.

Gordon observes that in the Roman world Mithra came to offer personal salivation:

> The god Mithras, creator and father of all, struggled with a white cosmic bull, which he finally overcame and killed. From the bull came all plant-life. Mithras was conceived as creator in so far as his actions released creative energy into the cosmos....In the West, the killing of the bull became the means of rebirth and salvation for man, presumably because the giving of life in the beginning was considered an allegory of the granting of life to sinful men (1972 96)

By leading a moral life was an important part of the path to salvation:

> On earth the initiate has the opportunity to shake off the weight of ...impurities by a combination of moral effort and knowledge revealed to him in the mysteries (Feguson 1970 121)

Thus, after coming to the Roman world from Persia, the cult of Mithras was "Romanized" and, to a large extent, it became the province of professional soldiers, although other men who spent long and lonely careers traveling without a family (such as sailors and merchants) also found Mithraism to be an attractive and comforting faith. Since membership provided camaraderie and a source of companionship, it was popular within its "target market" of single men far from home and it provided social as well as spiritual functions. Numerous Roman civil servants (many of whom were retired military men who were first introduced to the faith while serving in the army) also embraced the religion. Thus:

> It must not be forgotten that the cult of Mithra appealed especially to the soldier...To this was due the introduction of the mysteries into the army and the army was the principal... [method]...by which Mithraism passed into the Roman world (Schraff-Herzog 7 420.)

Catering primarily to soldiers and/or other single traveling men, Mithrasim evolved accordingly. "It was a man's religion in which women played no significant role" (*Encyclopedic Dictionary 1979.*) Thus, during the 1st century AD a powerful religion existed that catered to men, was associated with the military (the arm of Rome that repressed Christianity), and it was growing in wealth, prestige, and power throughout the Roman world. Distinct in some ways from the early church, Mithraism offered many of the same comforts that were promised by Christianity including moral guidance and the promise of an afterlife. In addition, various rituals and beliefs of Mithraism closely paralleled practices that emerged in the early Christian church.

Thus, Mithra sacrifices his life serving mankind only to be resurrected. Devotees, believed that they could earn a similar immortality. Thus, in very general ways, Mithraism made promises of eternal live that parallel those offered by the Christian faith. Rhetorically comparing Mithraism and Christianity, the *Standard Dictionary of Folklore and Mythology* asserts that if an ancient devote of Mithra could enter a modern Catholic church, he would feel right at home, finding:

> Baptism for the remission of sins, the symbolic meal of communion including consecrated wine, the sign on the brow, redemption, salvation, sacramentary grace, rebirth in the spirit and the promise of eternal life

Thus, Mithraism was a popular religion that had a strong moral message and promised eternal life to its members. It should also be mentioned that the Mithratic religion was well funded and benefited from excellent organization. Since Rome greatly respected and depended upon its army, furthermore, a religion that provided the military with courage and comfort would gain the respect and the support of the Roman leadership. In the 1st century, Mithraism was well positioned, professionally managed, and broadly based.

Rivalry with the Church

The growth of Mithraism and the writing of the gospels were contemporary events. Thus, "the first Christian century was the period of energetic propaganda [for Mithraism]" (*New Schaff-Herzog* 7 421.) Mithraism was emerging as an important Roman cult just as the Christian church was taking hold and the gospels were being written. Both Christianity and Mithrasim shared (at least superficial) many features and pursued roughly similar goals, including moral guidance and the promise of salvation/resurrection. It seems reasonable that under these circumstances, the church could come to view Mithraism as a distinct rival. Indeed, this appears to be the case. Thus, Sir James Frazer observes:

> There can be no doubt that the Mithraic religion proved a formidable rival to Christianity, combined as it did a solemn ritual with aspirations after moral purity and a hope of immortality. Indeed, the issue of the conflict between the two faiths appears for a time to have hung in the balance (1935 302.)

Some scholars doubt that Mithraism was a strong threat of Christianity (Toutain 1908, Duchesne-Guillemin 2003 744); such observations, however, appear to be the product of hindsight and not an opinion shared by early Christians. Ample evidence exists to demonstrate that a significant and conscious rivalry with Mithraism existed in the minds of the early leaders of the church. Although probably being hyperbolic, Ernest Renan, in a well known observation, asserts that if the Roman world had not become Christian, it probably would have become Mithratic (1923.) Even though Renan may have been overstating his case, enough evidence exists to support the thesis for Renan to be able to present it with a "straight face." Whatever inherent weaknesses might have existed within Mithraism, it was viewed as a real and powerful threat by early Christians.

Ancient Christian writers, for example, found Mithraism to be both distasteful and a menace to their own faith. They also acknowledged the rituals of Mithraism paralleled those of the church. Various ceremonies of Mithraism were at least superficially similar to those of the Christianity.

There was a communion service in memory of the farewell banquet of Mithras and the Sun; this included the drinking of wine (Feguson 1970 112.)

Perhaps this was merely a general or generic similarity:

> Some form of cult meal was one of the fundamental features of Greek religious festivals, and took the form of a meal devoted to, presided over, and shared with the gods (Kane 1975 321.)

In any event, Justin Martyr noted that:

> ...pagans dismiss [Christian] rituals with contempt and charge that Christians were simply copying what worshipers in the so-called mystery religions did every day (Pagels 2003 19.)

Indeed, the argument can be made that St. Paul may have gotten some ideas of ritual from Mithrasism or some other mystery cult:

Paul taught a doctrine of Baptism and Holy Communion that made Christianity structurally akin to the mystery religions (Bardon 1994 1997)

Although written over a century after the *Gospel of John*, Tertullian's "Prescriptions Against the Heretics" (circa 200) demonstrates that the church felt a heated rivalry with and loathing for Mithraism even while sharing many similarities with it:

[The Devil] apes even the divine sacraments in the idol-masters. Some he baptizes-his own believers, his own faithful. He promises the removal of sins by his washing, and if memory serves me [Tertullian's father was a Centurion] in this rite seals the soldiers on their foreheads. He celebrates...bread, brings on a representation of the resurrection. Tertullian circa 200 30.)

Such observations do not exist in isolation; Justin also defamed the religion while simultaneously observing the similarities between the rituals of Mithraism and the Eucharist:

The wicked demons in imitation handed down as something to be done in the mysteries of Mithra; for bread and a cup of water are brought out in their secret rites (Justin 287)

Thus, it appears that Mithraism had certain goals, strategies, and ceremonies that were similar to Christianity and that the church consciously viewed Mithraism as an enemy and threat.

The circumstances surrounding the decline and extinction of Mithraism provide additional evidence that Christianity feared Mithrasim. The last truly Pagan Emperor (besides Julian the Apostate and his aborted Pagan revival) was Diocletian who was responsible for the last great wave of persecutions against Christians that ranged from 303 until 313. He was a friend of the Mithratic religion and in 307 he dedicated an altar to Mithra (Jones 1926 759.)

Diocletian favored... [Mithraism] because it opposed Christianity. Under Constantine, imperial favor was withdrawn and Christianity demanded the repression of the cult (*New Schraff-Herzog* 1950 vol 7 423.)

In ancient times, therefore, the Christian church envisioned itself to be in conflict with Mithraism, a mystery cult that paralleled Christianity in some important ways. This ultimately led early church leaders to repudiate Mithraism and, after the political tides began to flow towards the church, repress it.

The Distinctiveness of Christianity

While Mithraism was a vital religion that dealt with the challenges of life, Christianity had its own strengths. On the one hand, Christianity was much more decentralized than Mithraism and this type of organization had its advantages. In addition, Christianity welcomed women. This not only doubled the possible number of converts, Christianity could be embraced by married couples. These strengths will be discussed.

Mithraism was a highly structured, well oiled machine. It was organized in grades of increasing authority that members understood and acknowledged. Mithraism clearly benefited from the Roman sense of authority and from the organizational principles that had developed in military life. It can be viewed with reference to the type of organizational chart that takes the form of a pyramid and where authority flows from the top to the bottom with few confusing variants or exceptions. In the Mithratic religion all members knew their place in the hierarchy and they were expected to act accordingly, even while struggling to climb ever higher up the organization and towards personal salvation.

The name "Mithra" actually means "contract." It would be fair to say that Mithraisism was a professionally managed, a legal corporation, and that its members exhibited a strong sense of discipline.

Christianity, in contrast, was highly decentralized even though it was envisioned as a universal organization. Each church was directed by a Presbyter, a leader with local decision making powers who had the authority to translate the tenets of the church in order to mesh with local conditions:

> The Presbyter by reason of his office ruled...his community, corrected abuses, was vigilant against false teachers...and was an authority, teacher and arbiter (Chiovare 1967 746.)

Such an arrangement is in stark contrast to Mithraism and its strong adherence to rank, hierarchy, and a universal structure.

This relative autonomy of individual churches probably gave Christianity a differential advantage over the cult of Mithraism when dealing with people who were not comfortable with a strict chain of command, reminiscent of military life. Christianity, furthermore, presents an image and vision of equality of the entire membership because Christian doctrine emphasizes that all people are sinners in God's eyes and that good deeds do not entitle anyone to God's grace. Paul's dictate of justification by faith (not works) portrays all people as equally in need of divine grace. This is in contrast to Mithraism that believed that people could, through hard work, graduate from grade to grade and, in the process, became superior to those on the lower rungs on the ladder to salvation. Devotees also believed they could win immortality as a result of their efforts.

Mithraism (as discussed above) was a highly authoritarian religion. It offered its adherents a positive replica of the hierarchy of the military experience (or other highly structured lifestyles) combined with an alternative to the abuses of power that sometimes occur in organizational life. Many other people, however, did not relish the structure of military life (or some other form of highly regimented existence); a religion based on military principles of rank would not have been attractive to these people. The more relaxed structure of Christianity, in contrast, would have been an attractive alternative to such individuals.

A second key aspect of Mithraism is that it was closed to women. According to Gordon, this arrangement seems to be an artifact of the fact that the religion was intertwined with military life. Nonetheless, the religion did enjoy fraternal relations with women of the cult of Cybele (Feguson 1970 112), probably because part the ceremonies of the two faiths were very similar (Smart 1984 280.) In any event, although Gordon concedes that many mystery cults had some sort of sexual restrictions, he maintains that Mithraism was much more rigid in this regard. He observes:

> There is a curious analogy in the refusal of the Roman army to countenance the legal marriage of soldiers until about 195 AD, a symbolic expression of the separation of camp and home. The religious life of Mithraism was more closely modeled on the values of camp than on home (98.)

Women, in contrast, were welcomed in the early Christian church. In the gospels, Jesus, provided comfort and encouragement to various women. As a result,

> Jesus enlarged and transformed women's possibilities for a full life. His manner and teachings elevated her status and gave her an identity and cause (Butler 1991 1415)

In addition, a number of women that are discussed in the gospels emerge as leaders who perform important functions (such as being the earthy mother of Jesus and being the first to discover that Christ has risen from the grave, etc.) Paul welcomed women collaborators (*Romans* 16 1, 3-5) and *Acts* mentions a husband/wife team engaged in evangelical work (*Acts* 18 26.) These are important roles even if occasional limits on women's participation are sometimes mentioned (as in *1 Corinthians* 14 33-8.)

Jesus also insisted that men and women should be judged on identical criteria and, that the double standard that had long prevailed in Jewish society needed to be set aside (Matthew 5 32, *Mark* 10 11-2.) Although it can be argued that the relationship of the early church towards women might not be "enlightened" according to today's standards, the early church provided a much more supportive environment than traditional Judaism and it was much more open to women than male-oriented Mithraism.

In his epistles, furthermore, St. Paul acknowledges that married couples can be loyal Christians, even though he seems to have preferred a celibate life of contemplation and service to Christ. In the 7th chapter of *1st Corinthians*, for example, Paul discusses marriage and even offers advice regarding martial problems. As a result, Christianity offered the people of the late 1st century a faith and salvation appropriate for both men and women and a religion that could form the basis of family life. Not only is this a far cry from the all-male ambience of Mithraism, it was also an arrangement that many people preferred.

As Elliott has observed, "Jesus turned to the...family as both basis and model for the movement...[This focus] was maintained by his followers after his death and well into the second century" (2003 205.) Wiedman, furthermore, emphasizes the family orientation of the church by pointing out that "Early baptism demonstrates children [were included within the] church in a way unparalleled among pagans" (186-92.)

Indeed, "Christianity had the advantage of...addressing itself to women as well as men-and women played a decisive part in its diffusion" (J. Duchesne-Guillemin 2003.)

Thus, Christianity was a distinctive religion and one that had strengths that were different from those of Mithraism, its rival. Mithraism was a strong, rich, and well organized religion that had earned the blessings of the Roman state. Nonetheless, it catered primarily to single men, was hinged around regimental life, and excluded women. Christianity, in contrast, was open to both sexes, could be embraced as a part of family life, and exhibited a degree of decentralization.

By spotlighting these differences, the emerging church would be better able to showcase the benefits being offered. In reworking the gambling soldiers incident, the *Gospel of John* appears to have done just that.

Juxtaposing Mithraism and Christianity

The background presented above demonstrates that in the late 1st century, Mithraism was a growing religion and that the early church viewed it as a serious threat. Although the two religions shared significant similarities, they were also very different. Possessing somewhat similar goals and rituals, (1) Christianity was more decentralized and (2) the early church welcomed women both as members and as leaders. Using this overview as an orientation, a discussion of the distinctiveness of the gambling soldiers incident in the *Gospel of John* is presented.

In *Matthew* (27:54), *Mark* (15:39), and *Luke* (23:34), the gambling soldiers are not closely connected to any other event associated with the crucifixion. In *John*, however, the portrayal of the gambling soldiers and the three Marys appear to be intertwined and consciously juxtaposed with each other. Thus, Raymond E. Brown observes: "The wording [of the gambling soldiers incident]...has suggested to some that John intended to contrast what the soldiers did with what Jesus' friends were doing in vss. 25–27" (Brown 1970 903.)

In spite of these internal clues, however, Brown is reluctant to believe that the author(s) of *John* intended to compare the gambling soldiers and the three Marys because "...this [is] quite unlikely, for there is no evidence that John thinks of the soldiers' actions of dividing the clothes as particularly hostile" (Brown 1970 903.)

Thus, Brown believes the only motive for the author(s) of *John* to juxtapose the gambling soldiers and the 3 Marys would be showcase the soldiers as particularly vile. But since the executioners of the era routinely appropriated the clothes of condemned prisoners, Brown argues that the ancients would not have been shocked or outraged by this behavior.

I agree with Brown that unless it can be shown that the author(s) of *John* sought to do more than merely depict the gambling soldiers as especially loathsome individuals, the juxtaposition theory cannot be defended. But, as I shall argue, if the author(s) wanted to use the comparison as a means of showing two competing religions together at the cross, the example emerges as significant. Mithraism, growing and prospering in the late 1st century, was viewed as a rival and as a threat to the early church; countering it had an important theological significance.

By merging the anecdote of the gambling soldiers with the depiction of the three Marys, a unified scenario emerges in which the soldiers can be envisioned as devotees of Mithra while the three Marys portray the power, strength, and potential of the struggling church. This important message provided the author(s) of *John* with a motive to reframe the story of the gambling soldiers in the way he did.

The Gambling Soldiers: Representative of Mithraism

The *Gospel of John* provides a much fuller account of the gambling soldiers incident than in the other gospels. Although *Biblical* critics have not agreed upon a reason for this more robust treatment of the anecdote, even a superficial glance suggests the editing may be purposeful and not a careless or pointless rewriting. The theory that the writing was conscious and purposeful is strengthened by the fact that throughout the *Gospel of John* the author(s) routinely reworked material that was found elsewhere in order for it to more clearly articulate and reinforce important theological issues.

For whatever reason, the author(s) of the *Gospel of John* provides a much more detailed account than is found in the synoptic record. In view of the fact that the author(s) usually wrote strategically, his choice to rework the incident was probably motivated by the goal to articulate an important religious point or principle. As demonstrated above, by juxtaposing Christianity with Mithraism he would have done so.

The band of gambling soldiers is a microcosm of Mithraism. First, it was all male (as was typical for that religion.) Secondly, it was composed of soldiers, the segment of society most identified with the religion. Thirdly, the activities of the soldiers (gambling) can be envisioned as an example of the "male camaraderie" that the cult encouraged and facilitated. Thus, at least superficially, the gambling soldiers resemble a Mithratic band pursuing its usual activities and pastimes, albeit while on the job (practicing a profession that, itself, was closely related to the cult.)

Without doubt, furthermore, John invests the gambling soldiers incident with a theological significance that is not found in the synoptic gospels. In specific, the *Gospel of John* belabors the point that the actions of the gambling soldiers ultimately fulfill one of God's prophesies. Thus, in *John* 19:24 we learn:

> They said therefore to one another, "let us not tear it, but cast lots for it, to decide whose it shall be"; that the scripture might be fulfilled, "THEY DIVIDED MY OUTER GARMETS AMONG THEM, AND FOR MY CLOTHINGS THEY CAST LOTS" (New American Standard Bible.)

According to the account as presented in the *Gospel of John*, the soldiers unwittingly contribute to God's plan by fulfilling one of his prophesies. Such an inadvertent contribution to God's plan on the part of the soldiers, of course, is paralleled throughout *John* (and the synoptic gospels) by the actions of the Pharisees (devotees of traditional Judaism, another rival religion) whose self-serving actions also unintentionally advance the divine agenda.)

If the gambling soldiers who advance God's cause are viewed as being devotees of Mithra, their actions and those of the Pharisees can be envisioned as parallel and reinforcing each other. Such amplification would have made the message of the *Gospel of John* much more powerful and compelling to late 1st century readers. If, in contrast, the soldiers are to be taken at face value (simply viewed as callous and ignorant enlisted men), the behavior is much more insignificant from a theological viewpoint. The view of random, insignificant individuals advancing God's plan, in contrast, is rather pedestrian and much less profound and compelling.

Because the author(s) of the *Gospel of John* was a strategic editor, it seems unlikely that he would have significantly changed the account of the gambling soldiers for no reason. If these soldiers are presented as members of a rival religion who unwittingly contribute to God's plan, the alteration would have made a significant statement about the power of God. This new emphasis would have been worthy of the editing that took place.

Even a superficial comparison of *John* and the synoptic gospels reveals that the author(s) spent considerable effort altering the story of the gambling soldiers in ways that suggest that their behavior was part of the divine plan. Because *John* provides many other evidences of God's will being achieved in ironic ways, another contrived example was hardly needed. If the story of the gambling soldiers was intended to express a key theological issue that was not adequately dealt with elsewhere, the changes would be meaningful and significant. By investing the gambling soldiers with the mantle of Mithraism, they, as the Pharisees, are depicted as devotes of a rival religion who inadvertently respond to God's will in ways that advance the church.

Presented in tabular form, the case for the argument that the Pharisees and the gambling soldiers both represent rival religions that unknowingly advance God's divine can be presented in Table 3.1:

Table 3.1: Pharisees and the Gambling Soldiers Compared

	Pharisees	Gambling Soldiers
Actions	The Pharisees follow the letter of the law (Jewish religious law) in their quest to take from Jesus what is legitimately his.	The gambling soldiers follow the letter of the law (prisoner's possessions revert to guards) in their quest to take from Jesus what is legitimately his.
Motivations	The Pharisees choose this course of action in order to selfishly enjoy the benefits of this world (maintain their social position), with little regard to larger and more profound issues.	The gambling soldiers choose their course of action in order to selfishly enjoy the benefits of this world (gain material possessions), with little regard to larger and more profound issues.
Result	God's will is fulfilled. Even though the Pharisees conduct their business to achieve their own private motives, they inadvertently act according to the divine plan.	God's will is fulfilled. Even though the gambling soldiers conduct their business to achieve their own private motives, they inadvertently act according to the divine plan.
Discussion	Both the Pharisees and the gambling soldiers can be viewed as representative of religions that rivaled the emerging Christian faith. *John* clearly affirms that the actions of both are orchestrated by God in order to achieve his purpose. In the late 1st century when *John* was first available, gentile believers were being challenged both by traditional Jews and by other rival sects, especially Mithraism. Portraying Mithraism in this way would have been a comfort to believers who were in competition with these powerful forces.	

Thus, by viewing the gambling soldiers as devotees of Mithra they can be compared to the Pharisees, members of another religion that also threatened *John*'s late 1st century readers. Being able to provide this comparison would have been a significant reason for the author(s) of *John* to edit the story of the gambling soldiers in the way he did, because if the soldiers are not viewed as representative of the Mithratic religion the power and implications of the incident are reduced. Since the author(s) of *John* was a very strategic writer, introducing significant changes for no reason would have been out of character.

The Three Marys Representing a Microcosm of the Church

As indicated above, some *Biblical* scholars have acknowledged that *John's* gambling soldiers appear to be juxtaposed with the three Marys. Because no theological reasons has been found for doing so, however, the alterations are dismissed as mere copyediting, motivated by no specific purpose. Nonetheless, the author(s) of *John* went to considerable effort in order to position the two groups in a way that invites a comparison.

In the synoptic gospels, for example, the three Marys are not standing at the foot of the cross (next to the gambling soldiers); they are found at the margins of the execution site. In *John,* the three Mary's are in close proximity to the cross and the gambling soldiers. This is quite a substantial change and the kind of alteration we would expect to have been strategically inspired.

In the *Gospel of John,* furthermore, the membership of this group is changed in a manner that more closely reflects the composition of the early church (as an organization that was open to both men and women,) This characteristic, as mentioned above, is one of the major benefits that made Christianity distinctive from Mithraism.

Both the Mithraic-like band of gambling soldiers and the microcosm of the early church, furthermore, advance the divine plan. The gambling soldiers unwittingly act according to a prophesy while the microcosm of the church follows Jesus' last instructions (the disciple Jesus loves is told to look after Jesus' mother) and render he comforts Jesus by giving him a last drink of wine before death. The Mithra theory offered here provides a compelling theological reason for the author(s) of *John* to portray a microcosm of the church tending to Jesus' wishes while he was still alive. By doing so, the church is juxtaposed to the gambling soldiers, representatives of Mithraism who unknowingly advance God's plan. Showcasing how both groups obey God's will in different ways is an important theological statement. And its importance rises when the gambling soldiers are portrayed as rivals to the church.

Looking at these two groups, certain similarities exist. Each is composed of four members. (The soldiers are four in number and the believers consist of the 3 Marys and the disciple that Jesus loved.) In addition, all are in close proximity to Jesus, being around him at the cross. The eight, furthermore, are obligated to be in attendance at the cross. The soldiers have been ordered to guard the site and to be sure the sentence is carried out. The Christians are obligated to comfort Christ and follow his last instructions.

Although there are similarities, differences also exist. The gambling soldiers are an all-male group, typical of a Mithratic band. These males are juxtaposed to a group of Christians composed of both sexes. Because a major "selling point" of early Christianity was its attitude towards women, this comparison would have been compelling to *John*'s readers.

The gambling soldiers are depicted as dupes who unknowingly carry out God's will. If identified with Mithraism, the power of the image grows profoundly. Analyzed in tabular form, we find in Table 3.2:

Table 3.2: The Church and Gambling Soldiers Compared

	Microcosm of Church	**Gambling Soldiers**
Religion	Overt Christians.	Followers of Mithra, the religion of soldiers.
Number	Three Marys and beloved disciple (A total of 4.)	A squad of soldiers. (A total of 4.)
Proximity	Close to Cross and the gambling soldiers. (This location is unique to *John*.)	Close to cross and close to the overt Christians (apparently the guards were assigned to prevent crowd interference.)
Composition	Women and men (3 Marys and beloved disciple.) A mixed group as typical of early Christian churches.	All men as would be typical of those following Mithra.
Concerns	Higher concerns. The promises and obligations of the Christian faith.	Low, worldly concerns (clothes taken from dying man.)
Vision	A vision of the promises made to serve God and comfort Jesus.	A short term vision only concerned with the here and now.
Role	Consciously involved with Jesus. Willingly adhering to his requests.	A pawn in God's plan. Inadvertently and unknowingly fulfilling a prophesy (This role is unique in *John*.)

Thus, the author(s) of *John* transformed the gambling soldiers into pawns who fulfill the divine agenda. A microcosm of the church is placed face to face with these soldiers. Both groups, in their own way, act in accordance to God's will. In view of the fact that the author(s) of *John* was a very strategic copywriter, it appears unlikely he would have gone to this trouble merely to show a bunch of lowly rabble juxtaposed with a few random Christians. If the gambling soldiers are viewed as a microcosm of Mithraism, a rival religion, the comparison is invested with a significant meaning. Such a literary devise will only work, however, if soldiers (devotees of Mithra) are depicted as being unable to see the significance of Jesus, but, nonetheless, act according to God's plan.

The Absence of the Centurion

In *Matthew*, *Mark*, and *Luke* there exists the story of the Centurion (a Roman officer probably supervising the execution of Jesus) who develops second thoughts and regrets the crucifixion. In the synoptic gospels, the inclusion of this scene could have served as a means of emphasizing that the church did not hold a grudge against Rome for killing Christ. Thus, the sacred texts of Christianity provide the account of a Roman officer showing remorse for the crucifixion (even if the less enlightened enlisted men are not so moved.) Such a portrayal can be seen as mirroring the portrayal of Pontius Pilate who is depicted as being reluctant to permit Christ's execution in the first place. The combined portrayals of Pilate and the centurion reinforce the premise that Christians did not blame Rome for killing Jesus and foster the conclusion that Christians were could not be easily incited to rise up against the state. Given the fact that Christian communities of the late 1st century were facing Roman repression and persecution provides a strong motive for the authors of the synoptic gospels to include such pro-Roman rhetoric in their sacred literature.

Indeed, the *New Testament* is filled with reassurances that Christians are not a threat to Rome. The most famous, perhaps, is the dictate urging people to "render up to Caesar what is Caesars". As indicated above, the whole treatment of Pontius Pilate can be read as a means of affirming that Christians blamed the Pharisees for Christ's death, not Rome. Critics and Biblical scholars have concluded that the *Gospel of Luke* and *Acts* were largely written in order to present Christianity in a way that could influence Roman officials in a positive manner.

Placing a Roman officer at the cross showing remorse for Jesus' death would further reinforce the thesis that the church blamed the Pharisees for the crucifixion, and, therefore, Rome had no reason to fear and repress the Christian faith. No doubt the leaders of the church felt the need to develop this chain of thought; after all, only a few years back, Nero blamed Christians for the fires that ravaged the City of Rome and harshly repressed the religion. Thus, the various authors of the synoptic gospels appear to have sent an "olive branch" to Rome in the form of a sorrowful and repentant centurion who represents Roman compassion, objectivity, and professionalism.

A careful comparison of the gospels reveals four distinct accounts of the centurion (if we include his absence as a distinct option.) In *Mark*, the first Gospel to be written (and as many critics have observed, the least strategically composed), the centurion observes "Truly this man was the Son of God" (15: 39.) In *Matthew*, a gospel written primarily for Palestinian Jews, the centurion is joined by the guards in affirming, "Truly this was the Son of God" (27: 54.)

In *Luke* (23:47), our centurion observes, "certainly this man was innocent", but he stops short of affirming a divine status for Jesus. Although these differences are subtle, they are significant and send distinct messages.

In *John*, the account of the centurion is not present. Eliminating the centurion story altogether is quite shocking, especially in view of the fact that the account provided a useful way to suggest that the church could exist in peace with the legal government because it did not blame Rome for Jesus' death.

Put in tabular form, a comparison of the four gospel's treatment of the centurion can be presented in Table 3.3:

Table 3.3: The Centurion at the Cross: Four Different Accounts

	Account	*Analysis*
Mark	Centurion says, "truly this was the son of God (15 39)	Centurion observes that Jesus is the son of God. Statement reinforces the portrayal of Pontius Pilate who o senses the significance of Jesus. Portrayal makes Rome appear less hostile.
Matthew	Centurion and guards say, "Truly this man was the son of God" (17 54)	Having the centurion and his men believe that Jesus was the Son of God portrays the entire Roman army in a positive light. In addition, this portrayal would make Christians appear less hostile towards Rome.
Luke	Centurion says "Certainly, this man was innocent" (23 47)	Luke presented a positive view of Christianity to Roman officials. Having the Centurion believe that Jesus was innocent would have portrays Christians as not blaming Rome for Jesus' death.
John	Remorseful Centurion not present	The author(s) of *John* edited out the remorseful centurion. Considering the benefits of portraying Rome in a positive light, this elimination must have served some important purpose.
Discussion	*John* drops the centurion scene altogether. Given the benefits in the centurion scenario, the author(s) of *John* must have edited out the centurion for some strategic reason.	

This comparison raises the question of "why would the author(s) of *John* remove the account of the centurion that had such a significant role in arguing that the Christianity was not a threat to Rome precisely at a time when the church faced significant Roman persecutions?"

If John presented the gambling soldiers as representatives of the Mithraic religion such a motive would have existed. Placing another soldier at the cross who shows remorse and perceives that Jesus is the son of God and/or is innocent would clearly confuse the issue and weaken the juxtaposition. An officer, furthermore, would have been a likely devote of Mithra because "the appeal of Mithraism to the highest ranks is beyond doubt" (Daniels 1975 272.) If the author(s) of *John* sought to depict soldiers as followers of Mithra, an excellent copywriting strategy would be to eliminate any other soldiers (especially leaders) who acted in a manner that contradicted the actions of this microcosm of Mithraism. Only by removing the centurion from the text of *John* can the gambling soldiers be portrayed as a microcosm of Mithraism. And in *John* the remorseful centurion is not present.

Conclusion and Discussion

The purpose of this essay is to carefully examine *John*'s reworking of the gambling soldiers incident that appears in the synoptic gospels and to propose a possible strategic reason why these editorial changes were made. Looking at the evidence and upon the circumstances facing the church in the late 1st century, one possible motive is to portray Mithraism, a religion that rivaled Christianity in the late 1st century, as unknowingly fulfilling the divine agenda. Such a portrayal of the gambling soldiers would have reinforced the earlier presentation of the Pharisees (devotees of another religion who unwittingly advanced God's purpose through their selfish behavior.) Although it is impossible to prove conclusively what the author(s) of the *Gospel of John* intended, the text is completely consistent with this theory.

Looking at the *Gospel of John* and the synoptic gospels, the following observations can be made:

1 In the synoptic gospels, the gambling soldiers incident is presented as a short, freestanding incident while in The *Gospel of John*, the gambling soldiers are portrayed in more detail and the soldiers seem to be closely associated with the three Marys in ways that invite a comparison.

2 In the *Gospel of John*, the three Marys are moved from the margins of the execution site to the foot of the cross in close proximity to the gambling soldiers.

3 Only in the *Gospel of John* are the three Marys joined with a male companion, making it a "mixed group" in a way that replicates the membership of the early church.

4. Only in *the Gospel of John* are the events of the gambling soldiers viewed as specifically contributing to the divine plan (fulfilling a prophesy.)

5. In the Gospel of John, the anecdote of the remorseful centurion (present in all the synoptic gospels) is removed even though that account provided a way to portray the Church as not blaming Rome, for Jesus' death (an important point to make during the repressions of the late 1st century.)

In spite of all these significant changes, current theories doggedly maintain that such alternations of the synoptic record are merely the fruit of non-strategic copyediting. This theory continues to be current because no strategic reason for making these changes has been proposed.

When the alterations are viewed as a means of transforming the non-descript gambling soldiers into representatives of Mithraism (a rival religion) a theological goal for these changes is offered. The devotees of this religion, furthermore, are shown as unwittingly and inadvertently acting in a manner that fulfills God's plan; this depiction gives the changes an even more theologically inspired purpose. Such a portrayal would have accomplished the following theological issues:

1 A rival, all male religion is juxtaposed with a microcosm of Christianity that is composed of both men and women.

2 The rival religion is portrayed as being unable to envision the significance of Jesus.

3, The microcosm of Christianity, in contrast, is portrayed as understanding the significance of Jesus.

4. The forces of Mithra are shown to be unwittingly acting in accordance to God's plan (fulfilling a prophesy) even though they are unaware that they are doing so.

5. In doing so, the behavior of the Mithratic band reinforces the image of the Pharisees, devotes of another rival religion who unknowingly advance the will of God through their selfish actions.

6 By removing the centurion, the *Gospel of John* provides no counter-example of a soldier (another likely Mithra devotee) who acts in ways that are inconsistent to the gambling soldiers and, thereby, dilutes the image.

As has long been acknowledged, the author(s) of *John* was a strategically oriented copywriter. Due to this fact, significant changes in the synoptic record (such as relocating the 3 Marys so they were in close proximity to the gamblers, and eliminating the remorseful centurion) were probably made for some specific purpose. Nonetheless, no reason has ever been found and, as a result, the changes are written off as trivial and non-strategic. That explanation, however, is unlikely because *John* was written in a careful and strategic manner.

In this essay, I have presented the case that the gambling soldiers represent members of the Mithratic religion that are compared and juxtaposed with a microcosm of the early church. In their actions, these soldiers inadvertently fulfill God's will. Conflicting references to a sympathetic soldier (the centurion) are eliminated in ways that prevent the message from being diluted, clouded, or confused.

Although it can never be proved conclusively what the author(s) of *John* was attempting to accomplish, this theory provides a plausible strategic motive regarding why the author(s) of *John* changed the portrayal of the gambling soldiers. This explanation, furthermore, is completely consistent with the text of *John* that exists and it fits with the cultural environment of the late 1st century when *John* was written. Given the force of the circumstantial evidence, this theory deserves to be considered as a serious explanation of why the author(s) of *John* altered the story of the gambling soldiers in the way he did.

References

Brandon, S. G . F (1994) "St Paul". in *Man, Myth, and Magic* Volume 14. (New Bellmore, New York: Marshall Cavendish)

Brown, Raymond E. (1970) The *Anchor Bible Gospel According to John* (xiii xxi) Introduction, Translation, and Notes by Raymond E. Brown. Garden City, New York Doubleday and Company)

Butler, Trent C. (1991) *Holman Bible Dictionary* (Nashville: Holman Bible Publishers.)

Chiovare, F. F. (1967) "Presbyter" in *the Catholic Encyclopedia* V 11 News York: McGraw Hill.

Cumont, Franz. (1956)*The Mysteries of Mithras.* (New York: Dover.)

Daniels, C. M. "The Role of the Roman Army in the Spread and Practice of Mithrasism" in Hinnells, John R. editor *Mithraic Studies: Proceedings of the First International Congress on Mithriac Studies* (Manchester: Rowan and Littlefield.) Pp249-274.

Duchesne-Guillemin, J (1967) Mithras and Mithraism in *New Catholic Encyclopedia* V 9 (New York: McGraw-Hill)

Duchesne-Guillemin, J (2003) Mithras and Mithraism in *New Catholic Encyclopedia* second edition V 9 774-5 (New York: Thompson-Gale.)

Eliott, John K. (2003) "The Jesus Movement was not Egalitarian, but Family Oriented." *Biblical Interpretation* V XI # 2 173-210.

Encyclopedic Dictionary of Religion volume f-n (1979) Washington, D. C. Corpus Publications.

Frazer, Sir James George (1935) *Adonis Attis Osiris: Studies in the History of Oriental Religion* 3rd edition v. 1 (New York:Macmillian)

Feguson, John (1970) *The Religions of the Roman Empire* (Ithaca, New York: Cornell University Press.)

Gnoli, Gherardo, (1987) "Mithra" in Eliade, Mircea, editor in chief *The Encyclopedia of Religion* v 9 (New York:Macmillian) 579-80

Gnoli, Gherardo, (1987a) "Mithraism" in Eliade, Mircea, editor in chief The *Encyclopedia of Religion* v 9 (New York:Macmillian) 580-82.

Gordon, R. L. (1972) "Mithraism and Roman Society: Social Factors in the Explanation of Religious Change in the Roman Empire" *Religion* V 2 1972

Hadas, Moses (1961) *Essential Works of Stoicism* edited by Moses Hadas with an introduction (New York: Bantam)

Herzog Encyclopedia of Religious Knowledge (1950) Baker: Grand Rapids, Michigan.

Hinnells, John R. (1975) "Editor's Introduction" in Hinnells, John R. *editor Mithraic Studies: Proceedings of the First International Congress on Mithriac Studies* (Manchester: Rowan and Littlefield.) Pp. xi-xvii.

Jones, H. Stuart (1926) "Mithraism" in *Encyclopedia of Religion and Ethics* edited by James Hastings V VIII (New York: Charles Scribner's Sons)

Justin "First Apology of Justin in *Early Christian Fathers* (1958) Volume 1 Cyril R. Richardson, editor and translator (Philadelphia: Westminister Press)

Kane, J. P. (1975) "The Mithraic Cult Meal in its Greek and Roman Environment" in Hinnells, John R. editor *Mithraic Studies: Proceedings of the First International Congress on Mithriac Studies* (Manchester: Rowan and Littlefield.) Pp. 313-351

Kipling, Rudyard (1990) "A Song to Mithras" *Rudyard Kipling: The Complete Verse* with a foreword by M.M. Kaye (London: Kyle Cathie Limited)

Mercatante, Anthony S. (1988) *The Facts on File Encyclopedia of World Mythology and Legend* (New York: Facts on File)

Merkelbach, R. (1994) "Mystery Religions" in *Man, Myth, and Magic* Vol 13 (New Bellmore, New York: Marshall Cavendish) 1807-11.

Momigliano, Arnaldo (1987) *On Pagans, Jews, and Christians* (Middletown, Connecticut: Wesleyan University Press)

McMullen, Ramsay (1969) *Constantine* New York: Harper Torchbooks)

New Interpreters Bible (1999) Nashville, Tennessee: Abingdon Press. V 9.

Pagels, Elaine, (2003) *Beyond Belief: The Secret Gospel of Thomas* (New York: Random House.)

Renan, Ernest (1923) *Marc Aureie et la Fin du Monde Antique* (Paris: Calmann-Levy.)

Smart, Ninian (1984) The Religious Experience of Mankind 3rd edition (New York: Scribners.)

Standard Dictionary of Folklore and Mythology (Funk and Wagnals)

Tertullian (ca 200 AD) "Perscriptions Against the Heritics" in *Early Latin Theology: Selections from Tertullian, Cyprian, Ambrose, and Jerome* (1956) Translated and edited by S. L. Greenslade (Philadelphia, Westminster Press.)

Toutain, J. (1908) "Le Culte de Mithra" in *Les Cultes Puiens dans l'empire romain* . Chapter 4 Volume 2 (Paris 1908–11.)

Ulansey, David (1989) *The Origins of the Mithaic Mysteries* (Oxford: Oxford University Press)

Walters, Vivenne (1974) *The Cult of Mithras in the Roman Provinces of Gaul* (Leiden: Brill.)

Wiedman, Thomas E. S. *Adults and Children in the Roman Empire* (New Haven: Yale University Press)

Chapter 4

The "Rich Fool" and Epicureanism

The parable of the "Rich Fool" that appears in the *Gospel of Luke* can be read as a repudiation of Epicurean philosophy, a force that challenged the early church while simultaneously rivaling Stoic philosophy, the orientation of many Roman civil servants. The following reading of the anecdote is presented as the most effective theory regarding why Luke uses the parable in the way he does.

The "Rich Fool" has long been examined by scholars; a representative sample of the analysis it has received includes Beavis (1997); Birdsall (1962); Lowery (1963); Malherbe (1996) Nickelsburg (1978-9); and Wright (2000.) The parable is often read as a commentary on exemplary behavior, an interpretation that goes back to at least to Julicher (1899 V.1, 114.) Embellishing this interpretation, others have offered more refined readings. Jones, for example, views the parable from the vantage point of the existential tradition (1999 142–62); Hultgren (2000 109) concludes the plotline explores what "one ought not to be like"; Whenham (1973 139) views the message as "a challenge to the rich establishment"; while Blomberg sees a commentary on the "spiritually damaging power of riches" (1990 266.) These, of course, are but representative examples of how various scholars have viewed the "Rich Fool"; it is not an exhaustive list.

Although a wide variety of interpretations exists, the cultural context of Palestine and Jewish traditions is often addressed as well as a focusing upon what the parable has to say about stewardship and greed.

Some of the observations made about the parable and its original context provide useful insights. The overt event that triggers Jesus' telling of the parable of the "Rich Fool", for example, involves a member of the crowd asking Jesus to help settle a partisan dispute. Various commentators have explained this situation with reference to the fact that people often viewed Jesus as a Rabbi: the kind of wise and notable person who routinely helped resolve such matters (see Jones 1999 144; Whenham 139 as representative examples of such perspectives.)

Although Jesus is invited to step in, he refuses to get involved and asks rhetorically, "Who appointed me a judge or arbiter over you" (*Luke* 12:14.)

Although he does not intercede in the dispute, the situation provides the occasion for Jesus to recite his parable.

The story concerns a man who enjoys spectacular financial success and anticipates that he will be able to enjoy his wealth for many years. Instead of sharing the bounty of good fortune with others, this lucky individual builds bigger barns to store his fortune so it will be available to provide him with the good things in life during the foreseeable future. *Luke*'s Jesus tells us that this man planned to "eat, drink, and be merry" (*Luke* 12: 19.) Hultgren assumes that this phrase reflects, refers to, or was inspired by *Old Testament* precedents: a technique that Jesus often employed during his ministry. Hultgren asserts, "The final saying (eat, drink, and be merry) is commonplace. Similar sayings appear elsewhere in Jewish tradition (LXX Eccl 8: 15) having the same Greek verbs..." (2000 107.)

As the parable continues, the man unexpectedly dies. *Luke* tells us, "...God said to him, 'You fool. This very night your soul is required of you; and now who will own what you have prepared'". (*Luke* 12: 20.) This is followed by Jesus using the example of the "Rich Fool" to encourage his audience to build up permanent riches in heaven. (*Luke* 12: 33.)

Thus, the "Rich Fool" is often viewed as a parable of exemplary behavior (albeit exemplary behavior portrayed via a negative example.) As indicated above, this tradition of interpretation, which goes back to Julicher, typically focuses upon local Palestinian cultural lore and the Jewish heritage. Such perspectives form the usual foundation for analysis and exegesis.

In this regard, Hultgren (2000 105) observes:

["The Parable of the Rich Fool"] has an antecedent in Jewish literature from the second century B.C. (*Sirach* 11:18–19), although the later is not in the form of a parable...It is possible that the parable has been inspired by this passage in some way, even if it is not directly dependent upon it. Both the passage from Sirach and the parable stand within the wisdom tradition of Israel."

Thus, the parable of the "Rich Fool" tends to be viewed from within the context of Palestine culture and Jewish religion as a commentary regarding noble behavior.

A Larger Context

While the *New Testament* can be read with reference to Palestinian culture, the Jewish tradition, and the emerging Christian message, it was also created within a wider context that needs to be acknowledged. As is universally recognized, the Roman world of the later 1st century was a spiritual battleground where a wide variety of religions and philosophical systems (including stoicism and Epicureanism) competed with each other for the hearts and minds of the people.

This essay focuses upon this heterogeneous religious, ethical, and spiritual context that existed when Luke wrote. Doing so is particularly important because Luke (who records this parable) was actively involved in the larger world and he was not merely an uninformed provincial from Palestine. Luke was a medical doctor and his Greek is excellent, indicating he was an informed sophisticate. Luke, furthermore, wrote the *Gospel of Luke* and the *Acts of the Apostles*) in order to favorable impress Roman officials and civil servants. As a result, while his writing inevitably deals with Christian issues, Luke was also writing in an idiom that would resonate with influential Romans who could help advance the cause of the church.

Viewed from such a vantage point, this analysis demonstrates how the "Parable of the Rich Fool" can be read as a hostile critique of the Epicurean philosophical system that in the late 1st century formed a powerful ethical and spiritual alternative to Christianity and rival philosophical systems, such as stoicism. Thus, the parable (as presented by Luke) can be legitimately viewed as a commentary upon a rival vision of life, not merely as a call to exemplarity behavior (as Julicher and Hultgren suggest) or as a reworking of materials that had long existed within the Jewish traditions of Palestine. While not denying that multiple influences may simultaneously exist, a strong argument can be made that Luke was consciously rebutting the Epicurean tradition when he presented his unique and distinctive account of Jesus' "Parable of the Rich Fool."

Other illusions to Epicureanism exist in the *New Testament*. Norman DeWitt (1954), for example, convincingly argues that the phrase "their god is the belly" that appears in *Philippians* 3: 19 (Dewitt 1954 chapter 2) refers to the hedonistic tendencies attributed to Epicureans. In this regard, DeWitt quotes Epicurean writer Metrodorus who states, "The pleasure of the stomach is the beginning and the root of all good, and in this the things of wisdom and the refinement of life have their standard of reference." Indeed, even today, the term "Epicurean" is often used to identify lovers of fine food. DeWitt argues that although Paul was somewhat critical of Epicureanism, he was favorably impressed by it in many ways. As will be argued below, Luke, in contrast to Paul, sought to dismiss Epicurean philosophy in a hyperbolic and stereotypic manner.

In arguing this case, the theory that Luke was (directly or indirectly) writing to Roman officials (who tended to be opponents of Epicureanism) is embraced. A classic perspective emphasizes that Luke wrote to a member of the Roman civil service in order to encourage better treatment of the church. Today, of course, this theory is sometimes questioned since evidence exists that indicates that Luke may have been instructing a Christian audience on how to reason with Roman leaders. In either case, however, Luke's arguments would have helped present Christianity to the Roman civil service in a positive light. The only difference is that in one theory asserts Luke directly wrote to Roman officials while in the other he was coaching other Christians regarding how to deal with important Romans. This observation is discussed more fully in Chapter 2 above.

An overview of Epicureanism is necessary in order to show how Luke used the parable to discredit Epicureanism in order to impress Roman civil servants. Before presenting this evidence, it is necessary to underscore that a wide variety of scholars in recent years have recognized that various *New Testament* texts deal with Epicureanism. This literature includes a wide variety of critical studies including DeWitt (1954), Malherbe (1999), Tomlion (1997), Kirby (2003), etc. The argument that the authors of the *New Testament* were aware of Epicurean (an important Greek) philosophy is bolstered by the fact that it is widely recognized that the *Gospel of John* makes pointed and powerful illusions to stoicism, another influential Greek philosophy that was a strong rival to Epicureanism. Paul's discussions of gentiles who intuitively possess the law that they were never taught (*Romans* 2:14), furthermore, closely reflects a stoic orientation. John's use of the term "word" that dominates the first two verses of his gospel is inspired by stoic usage and perspectives. St. Paul, furthermore, was comfortable referring to pagan religions (as in his speech at Mars Hill.) Thus, the *New Testament* contains many references to rival religious and spiritual systems that existed in the larger Roman world.

This paper can be seen as an extension of other studies that examine the impact of Epicurean philosophy upon the New Testament (although the author is aware of no other example of exegesis that analyzes "the Parable of the Rich Fool" in terms of the Epicurean tradition.)

The Stoic and Epicurean Traditions

Scholars generally discuss the emergence of the Epicurean tradition (as well as its rival, Stoicism) with reference to changes that were triggered by the conquests of Alexander the Great. Before Alexander, the Greeks tended to center their life around the local community; people identified with their hometowns and looked to their city-state of origin for psychological comfort. Alexander's conquests, however, destroyed the power and independence of the city states, a situation that transformed the way in which the Greeks related to the world and to themselves. Alexander's conquests, furthermore, greatly expanded the Greek sphere of influence and, as a result, many "Greek" cities were established over the wide-ranging territory that had been brought under a Greek sphere of influence. This situation caused many ambitious Greeks (at least those who were forced to seek economic opportunities overseas) to abandon their homeland. When this happened, the Greeks became increasingly alienated and cut off from the civic heritage that had traditionally formed the center of life and previously served as a primary source of comfort and personal identity.

As the original "Hellenic" world was replaced by the broader and more international "Hellenistic" environment, the Greek people began to abandon their traditional "collective" orientation and develop an emotional self-sufficiency that could help them deal with the fact that they were becoming increasingly alienated, isolated, and alone. People sought a new form of independence and self-sufficiency to replace the dependence upon their city state that had been lost: the term "ataraxia" refers to this new system of life and the peace of mind it offered. During this era of cultural transformation, both Epicureanism and stoicism emerged as systems that were poised to provide the independence and self-sufficiency that was needed when the city states could no longer provide security, identity, and psychological comfort. As the emerging Hellenistic world transformed Greek life, self-image, and personal identity, the stoic and the Epicurean systems helped people to cope with the new realities of life.

While these two philosophical schools responded to similar pressures, they were in heated disagreement with each other. The stoics envisioned people living in a world that is bigger than they were and, as a result, individuals were encouraged to accommodate themselves to it. Thus, the stoic system helped people gain self sufficiency and atraxia by teaching them to accept what inevitably happens in the belief that the world is basically good, even though bad or hurtful things often occur.

> Stoicism became a "popular philosophy" in a way that neither Platonism nor Aristotelianism never did. In part this is because Stoicism, like its rival Epicureanism, addressed the questions that most people are concerned with and in very direct and practical ways. It tells you how you should regard death, suffering, great wealth, poverty, power over others and slavery. (Stanford 2006 15.)

Stoic philosophy focuses upon (1) accepting the dictates of fate and (2) working within the parameters of nature in order to merge with it. By accepting the inevitable and becoming one with nature, the stoics believed that people could achieve a kind of immortality; this vision provided comfort. As time went by, stoic philosophy developed a strong moral and altruistic bent. Although stoicism originally encouraged people to remain distinct from the world, under the Romans it was transformed into a creed that provided guidance to people who were active in the world. As a result, stoic philosophy became a quasi religion and an ethical system that was very popular among the Roman civil service. Marcus Aurelius (a highly regarded Roman emperor who ruled from 161 to 180 AD), for example, was a major stoic philosopher.

While the stoics came to focus upon acting in ways that accept the power of nature and acknowledge mankind's subservient place within it, the Epicureans focused on the individual. The most basic and primary orientation of the Epicurean system involved the twin preoccupations of (1) increasing pleasure and (2) reducing pain. For Epicurus the aim of life was pleasure and the highest pleasure was the absence of pain. Epicurus, incidentally, believed the pleasure of the mind was preferable to that of the body. He also believed in moderation; thus popular depictions of Epicurean philosophy as overly hedonistic, self-indulgent, and lustful do not truly represent its orientation. Nonetheless, while stoicism focused on the larger world and emphasized a moral responsibility to others, Epicurean philosophy centered upon the individual and offered strategies for maximizing the individual's pleasure while minimizing pain.

Besides focusing on individual comfort and personal wellbeing (measured with reference to some kind of pain vs. pleasure ratio) Epicurean dogma (1) denied the belief in an afterlife and (2) insisted that the Gods (although they might exist) do not intervene in human affairs and, therefore, they are of no concern to mankind.

While stoicism emphasized that the human spirit should seek immorality by merging with and contributing to nature, the Epicurean system denied the existence of any afterlife. In his "letter to Menoeceus", for example, Epicurus (founder of Epicurean philosophy) states, "death, the most terrifying of ills, is nothing to us since so long as we exist death is not with us, but when death comes, then we do not exist. It does not then concern either the living or the dead, since for the former it is not and the latter are no more" (Oates 1940 31.)

Because Epicureanism insists that the soul dies with the body, it maintains that death does not lead to an afterlife and people have no reason to fear it.

This theory was further bolstered by Lucretius (95–55 BC), a Roman poet who was a powerful apologist for the Epicurean system. He wrote *De Rerun Nature (On the Nature of Things)* as a means of explaining the tenets of Epicurean philosophy in a literary and poetic manner. This work was widely circulated during the 1st century when the gospels were written. After introducing a materialistic conception of reality in Books 1 and 2, Lucretius goes on in Book 3 to provide various arguments that the soul is mortal. He observes, for example:

> ... the mind is begotten along with the body and grows up together with it and becomes old with it...when the body has been shattered by the mastering might of time and the frame has drooped with its forces dulled, then the intellect halts, the tongue dotes, the mind give way...It naturally follows that [at death] the whole nature of the soul is dissolved (Oates 1940 124.)

Thus, the Epicurean system completely rejects any vision of immortality or eternal life. As a result of this belief (or lack of belief), the attention of Epicureans was directed to the here and now, not to projections of an afterlife.

Epicurus furthermore, believed that although the gods may exist they do not become involved in human affairs. This perspective is further bolstered by Lucretius in Book 6 of *On the Nature of Things* where he presents rational explanations for a wide array of natural phenomena (such as the weather, volcanoes, etc.) in ways that undercut the belief in divine intervention.

Epicurus went on to conjecture that mankind tended to anthropomorphize the gods and falsely view them accordingly. Thus he says in his "Letter to Monoeceus":

> [The gods] are not such as the many believe them to be...And the impious man is not he who denies the gods of the many, but he who attaches to the gods the beliefs of the many. For the statements of the many about the gods are not conceptions derived from sensation [empirical observation], but false suppositions [that assert that]...the greatest misfortunes befall the wicked and the greatest blessings [to] the good by gift of the gods. For men being accustomed always to their own virtues welcome those like themselves, but regard all that is not of their nature as alien (Oates 1940 30.)

Thus, Epicurus asserts that (contrary to the beliefs of Christianity and various pagan sects) the gods/God do not punish the evil or reward the just. Because the gods do not become involved in human affairs, Epicurus concludes that there is no reason to either fear them or seek their favor.

An analogy can be drawn between this Epicurean belief and the tenets of "deism", a conception of reality that was popular among intellectuals during the 18th century. Deism did not deny the existence of God, but it did affirm that once God created the universe, he left the scene and allowed this complex "machine" he had created to operate on its own without further divine intervention. As a result of this belief, the deists concluded that that God was not an active participant within human affairs.

Thus, both stoicism and Epicureanism helped people gain psychological comfort in a changing world. Although both provided self-sufficiency and independence, these systems did so in opposite ways; Stoicism focused upon the larger world, urged people to adjust to it, and asked people to accept pain and hardship while the Epicurean system concentrated how the individual could maximize pleasure and minimize pain. Discussed in tabular form, the key tenets of the Epicurean system can be portrayed in Table 4.1:

Table 4.1: Tenets of Epicureanism

Issue	Description	Analysis
Focus on comfort	The Epicurean system focuses upon how individual people can maximize pleasure and minimize pain.	According to Epicureanism, the goal of life should center upon maximizing pleasure and minimizing pain. Other issues and concerns are marginalized
No after life	The Epicurean system was materialist and empirical and used science to conclude that there is no life after death.	By Denying an afterlife, the feat of future pain was reduced, helping people to concentrate on the here and now.
God uninvolved	While not denying the existence of the gods, the Epicurean system asserted that the gods do not become involved in human affairs	Denying that the gods become involved in human affairs, Epicureanism concluded that they were not a source of either pleasure or pain. As a result, people were counseled to be indifferent to the gods.
Discussion	The Epicurean system provided a way for people to cope with a changing world. Because the philosophy focused on the individual, was centered upon the here and now, and discounted the impact of the gods, it helped people develop a greater sense of self-sufficiency. Many people used this system to find psychological peace and comfort.	

Thus, the Epicurean system provided a well thought out philosophy of life. Scholars generally conclude that while the intellectual foundation of stoicism evolved over many generations, adjusted to circumstances, and became eclectic, the Epicurean system developed a strong and consistent intellectual superstructure that formed a formidable system of thought that was nearly air-tight and did not evolve in ad hoc ways in order to respond to evolving circumstances and intellectual developments.

The Epicurean system, however, was in significant conflict with both stoicism and the emerging Christian tradition. Each of the key points of the

Epicurean system discussed above, for example, was stoutly rejected by both the stoics and the Christians. Although the stoics and Christians dismissed Epicureanism for different reasons, they stood shoulder to shoulder in their repudiation of the Epicurean world view. A brief overview of these rebuttals is presented in Table 4.2:

Table 4.2: Rebuttals of Epicureanism

Issue	Christian-centered rebuttals	Stoic-Centered Rebuttals
Focus on comfort	Epicureanism focuses on personal comfort. Christianity encouraged just and pious behavior no matter what pain it caused.	Stoicism focused on suffering and learning to tolerate it. Pain is more bearable when realizing how it fits into the broader plan.
No life after death	Christians believed that the soul survives after death. Those who are saved will enjoy paradise while those who did not will suffer hell.	Stoics believed the world is good. By contributing to it people can merge with nature to gain collective immortality. Others suffer accordingly
God not involved	Christians believed in a personal God that was involved in human affairs.	Stoics believed in the overarching forces of nature impact human affairs.
Discussion	Both Christianity and stoicism were in direct conflict with Epicureanism. Although these two systems of belief were different, they both opposed the key tenets of the Epicurean system and rejected that rival system.	

Detractors have often depicted Epicurean philosophy as overly hedonistic, using the resulting "straw man" logic to dismiss it. These depictions, however, are hyperbolic and unfair. As Oates (1940 xvii) observes:

> Various philosophers and critics in the history of Western European thought have made the mistake of supposing that the materialistic monism of Epicurus is an ignoble philosophy. It can confidently be asserted that such is not the case, for what Epicurus sought primarily to do was to rid men from certain besetting fears which tainted their lives, namely the fear of the gods which led to superstitions... and fear of death with all its concomitants...

Epicurus also urges a careful discrimination among the several pleasures and categorically rejects such pleasures as may be momentarily intense but which are followed by attendant pain. Hence, he urges for the principle of the mean, or moderation, joys that accrue from friendship, and the advantages of living a simple life.

The Epicurean system, therefore, was a powerful philosophical school that helped many people in the Greek and Roman communities of the 1st century AD to cope with the pressures they faced. These people received comfort by ignoring the gods, denying an afterlife, and focusing on a temperate life that sought to gain pleasure and avoid pain. In doing so, however, the system emerged as the enemy of both Christianity and stoicism.

Luke's Redactionary Approach

This paper argues that Luke consciously orchestrated the materials at his disposal in order to favorable impress members of the Roman civil service. As Walle has argued (2001 43):

> The *Gospel of Luke* was overtly and consciously written to influence Roman officials and the Roman Government (which had at times been hostile to Christianity.) Gaining the sympathy of the central government, of course, would clearly advance the goals of the church. *Luke* is best viewed as a public relations document created for lobbying purposes among Roman leaders. Biblical scholars maintain that Luke was specifically written for a Roman official named Theophilus and that the author [Luke] consciously hoped that a positive overview of the church, presented to this influential civil servant, might engender more favorable treatment.

In order to achieve this goal:

> Luke and *The Acts of the Apostles* (originally written as volume 2 of *Luke*) dealt with Romans in a most cordial manner. Luke belabors the point that Pontius Pilate, the Roman administrator involved in Christ's execution, was not responsible for the verdict and that Pilate actually tried to intercede on Christ's behalf. Pilate's wife, furthermore, refers to Christ as a "just man" and Luke's Pilate attempts to facilitate the release of Christ on numerous occasions. Such content was vital to Luke's message as he wished to show that Christians did not hold a grudge against Rome for the death of Christ (Walle 2001 44.)

This redactive interpretation of Luke's writing (that is built upon in this paper) seeks to understand the *Gospel of Luke* with reference to Luke's target audience. Since Willi Marxen's seminal work (1954), redaction criticism has emerged as a powerful tool of Biblical scholarship that depicts authors as more than passive conveyers of information. Redaction criticism expands beyond form criticism (that focuses on genres, techniques of oral transmission, and how they impact texts), by exploring how specific writers used (and/or possibly abused) the materials at their disposal in order to develop and maintain a specific chain of thought.

Without doubt, authors strategically work and rework the materials at hand in order to suit their needs and to achieve their goals. Even though the individual authors of the *New Testament* may have felt strong restraints to remain true to their sources, they would still have had "wiggle room" to edit and embellish their accounts in some kind of strategic manner. Thus, the *Gospel of Matthew* is often viewed as a gospel that was written for evangelical work among the Jews (and emphasizes Jewish themes as a result) while, Luke recast his materials in order to influence the Roman civil service.

While the conscious goals, perspectives, and visions of an author often exert a strong impact, scholars and critics also understand that other forces are at play when people write. Psychological critics, for example, routinely focus upon the fact that authors might not be aware of the full implications of their work and may be expressing repressed feelings, intuitive beliefs, covert attitudes etc. Thus, the true message of a piece of literature may lie in its ability to reveal what lies below the level of consciousness, not overt goals and rational actions. Other methods of analysis, such as structuralism and poststructuralism, also tend to discount the author's avowed and conscious intentions.

Nonetheless, when used with care and when not pushed beyond their appropriate applications, methods that explore the author's conscious intent can provide useful insights. Redaction criticism (Biblical scholarship's tools for dealing with the author's conscious intent) and related methods (such as those used here) are appropriate when used in responsible ways.

In line with the goals of redaction criticism, this paper expands Walle's depiction of Luke as a strategically oriented author by arguing that Luke depicted Epicurean philosophy in a hostile manner in order to influence Roman officials who (typically being stoics) tended to view Epicureanism as a significant rival.) Thus, the "Parable of the "Rich Fool" drew positive parallels between stoicism and Christianity in ways that underscored their mutual opposition to Epicureanism, a philosophy that they both feared and rejected.

Luke wrote in the hope of gaining more favorable treatment from the Roman civil service at a time when Christians feared Roman reprisals. The atrocities of Nero were within human memory and Luke, no doubt, hoped such events would not be repeated. Luke's generous treatment of Pontius Pilate subtly argues away the notion that Christians hated Rome for executing Christ. In the "Parable of the Rich Fool", Luke goes beyond dismissing the fear that Christians are anti-Roman to show Christianity rejecting Epicureanism in ways that parallel the critiques of stoicism. Since stoicism was the ethical foundation the Roman civil service, this parallel would have favorably impressed important governmental officials who ultimately made and enforced public policies regarding Christianity.

Viewed from this redaction criticism perspective, Luke had a strong strategic motive to present "the Parable of the Rich Fool" in the way he did; by doing so, he encouraged Roman civil servants to treat Christians in a kinder and gentler way.

A Comparison with the *Gospel of Thomas*

One of the classic ways to analyze *New Testament* texts (including the parables) is to compare a passage with parallel versions that are found elsewhere. By doing so, differences that exist in variant texts may reveal the goals of the particular author, explore the distinctiveness of specific audiences being addressed, demonstrate partisan views that are being showcased, etc. When looking only at the *New Testament*, this kind of analysis is impossible because the "Parable of the Rich Fool" exists only in *Luke*. A variant version of the parable, however, is found within the *Gospel of Thomas*. *Thomas* was apparently originally written in Greek and fragments of the gospel written in Greek were discovered in the 19th century. A complete version of the text in Coptic was discovered among the Nag Hammadi library in 1945 and since that time it has come to be viewed as an invaluable non-canonized source document regarding early Christianity.

The Gospel of Thomas (although not in the Christian canon) has increasingly gained prestige among Biblical scholars. The Jesus Seminar, for example, has treated the *Gospel of Thomas* on a par with the gospels of the Christian canon (*Matthew, Mark, Luke,* and *John*) in its attempts to ferret out authentic saying that can be attributed to Jesus. Because the credibility of the Jesus Seminar has been called into question by some scholars (consider the assertion that it might be sacrificing rigorous research for the sake of publicity as suggested by White 1998), it is not being dealt with as authoritative here. Although this paper has no opinion (pro or con) regarding the Jesus Seminar, the fact that it, a major research initiative, views the *Gospel of Thomas* alongside the canon is a precedent for the method used in this analysis (in which a parable from *Luke* is juxtaposed with a variant that appears in *Thomas*.) Various individual research efforts have employed the same tactic. Thus, this essay exists within the mainstream of Biblical scholarship.

Considerable debate exists regarding the date when the *Gospel of Thomas* was written. Some scholars (such as Elaine Pagels) argue for a 1st century writing (i.e. around the same time that the other gospels were composed.) In her *Beyond Belief* (2003), for example, Pagels suggests that certain passages in the *Gospel of John* appear to be responses to the *Gospel of Thomas*. Such an interpretation implies that the author(s) of the *Gospel of John* would have been aware of the *Gospel of Thomas* when that gospel was written—hence an early date is proposed.

Those who argue for that the *Gospel of Thomas* was created at a later date are swayed by the apparent Gnostic leanings which they believe were not a strong force in earlier times. Advancing such a chain of thought, Graham Stanton argues that The *Gospel of Thomas* is a Gnostic document and "removing the Gnostic veneer will never be easy" (2002 129.)

This paper has no opinion regarding when the *Gospel of Thomas* was written, although I am impressed by Pagel's arguments. What is most important is not the actual date but a comparison of the parable as it appears in the two texts. While Luke wrote strategically in order to present a specific point of view (and he provides a considerably expanded version of the parable in the process), the *Gospel of Thomas'* version is short and it does not show the same degree of redactive manipulation by its author. Thus, Funk and Hoover (1967 508) insist: "As a single, unelaborated tale the *Thomas* version [of the "Parable of the Rich Fool"] retains more of the characteristics of orally transmitted tradition and is probably an earlier form of the parable than *Luke*'s."

Funk and Hoover (who hope to tease out the original words of Jesus), suggest that Thomas' version of the parable was the first to be written down and it might be a more accurate reflection of the way Jesus spoke. If this is true, the degree of redactive manipulation by the author of *Thomas* will be less than in *Luke*: an author who apparently rewrote an earlier account for a specific strategic purpose. Luke, therefore, did not merely repeat what already existed in a purely objective and nonpartisan manner.

It appears, furthermore, that in the *Gospel of Luke* the "Parable of the Rich Fool" has been edited in order for the author to emphasize points that were important to the message he was providing. Thus Koester observes: "There are two secondary features in the narrative of Luke: the conclusion and the moralizing discourse. Both are missing in Thomas's version which presents the story in the more original form" (1990 98.)

This editing, furthermore, may have actually undermined the power of the original story. Thus, Jeremias notes: "The closing sentence, too, of the parable of the Rich Fool...must be an addition; it is missing from the *Gospel of Thomas* [this addition] gives a moralizing meaning to the parable, which blunts the sharp edge of its warning" (1963 106.)

While the date of composition of the *Gospel of Thomas* and the influences upon it are matters of speculation and controversy, there is general agreement about its format. Each of the gospels in the canon is written in narrative form.

Because they tell a story, various elements, sayings, motifs, etc. in the canonized gospels are more likely to have been "worked into the plotline." The *Gospel of Thomas* is different; while sharing much of its content with the gospels of the canon; it does not have a tight and well integrated structure. *Thomas*, in contrast to the gospels of the canon, can best be viewed as a collection of sayings and incidents that exist in a largely free standing manner and, as a result, they are not interconnected with each other in ways that serve the greater strategic purpose of the author.

This "scrapbook format" of the *Gospel of Thomas* suggests that the author was compiling materials that were available and that they do not appear to be overly manipulated, edited, or embellished for some partisan or holistic purpose (as would be the case in a situation where materials were subordinated to fit into a plotline being presented by the author.)

The version of the "Rich Fool" that exists in the *Gospel of Luke*, therefore, shows more signs of being manipulated by the author than the parallel version that exists in the *Gospel of Thomas*. As Jeremias observes, furthermore, there is evidence that Luke may have (wittingly or unwittingly) sacrificed some of the power of the parable in order to adjust the text to better serve his purposes.

Luke's Version and its Anti-Epicurean Focus

Various Biblical scholars have recognized that the protagonist in the "Parable of the Rich Fool" is a hedonist (see, for example, Malherbe 1996) and researchers routinely recognize that Epicurean philosophy was hedonistic. Luke' portrayal of the "Rich Fool" closely parallels the way in which Epicureans were stereotyped. This alone, however, does not prove that Luke presented his portrayal of the "Rich Fool" with Epicurean philosophy in mind.

One of the clichés of Epicurean philosophy, of course, is that it encourages devotees to "eat, drink and be merry for tomorrow they may die." While the true Epicurean perspective is much more robust, thoughtful, and complicated (as well as being less hedonistic) than this derogatory oversimplification suggests, detractors have often dismissed Epicureans accordingly. The strong parallel between the depiction of the "Rich Fool" in Luke and the common stereotype of the Epicurean has not gone unnoticed within Biblical scholarship. Thus, Bernard Brandon Scott has observed: "[The protagonist of "the Parable of the Rich Fool"]...identifies himself as an Epicurean" (Scott 2002 93.) In view of the fact that *Luke*'s Jesus uses the phrase "eat, drink, and be merry", this parallel to Epicureanism is even stronger and appears to be an overt reference.

In spite of the similarities between Jesus' portrayal of the "Rich Fool" in *Luke* and popular dismissals of Epicurean philosophy, scholars have tended to overlook these parallels. As a result, the versions of *Luke* and *Thomas* are viewed as having an identical message; as a result, the impact of redactive editing on Luke's part tends to be ignored or under-emphasized. Thus, Gerd Lundemann equates the *Luke* and *Thomas* versions of the parable in spite of their obvious differences. He observes: "This exemplary narrative [of *Thomas*] is related to *Luke* 12:16-20. But the economic circumstances are slightly different...The meaning of the two parables however, is the same. Sudden death can overtake even the shrewdest of men" (622.)

This paper disagrees with such equating and suggests that recasting the "Rich Fool" as an Epicurean may have been a calculated action on Luke's part because he wanted to impress Roman civil servants who were stoic and, thereby, rivals and opponents of Epicureanism.

Thus, while this analysis builds upon earlier observations that the "Rich Fool" has Epicurean tendencies (Scott 2003, for example), the argument goes beyond earlier scholarship by suggesting that Luke wrote in a redactive manner in order to emphasize these similarities in a manner that would positively influence his chosen target audience (Roman civil servants.)

In making this case, the number of key issues to be addressed include: (1) Luke wrote in order to impress Roman officials, (2) Roman officials tended to be stoics who viewed Epicureans as a rival philosophy, (3) Luke presented his parable in a way that would impress stoic civil servants, and (4) Luke took an earlier text (represented by the *Gospel of Thomas'* version) that provided a generic moral message regarding greed and stewardship and transformed it into an attack upon a specific philosophical position (Epicureanism.) These issues will be discussed.

Roman Officials: Luke's Target Audience

As indicated above, Luke wrote in order to positively influence a particular target audience: members of the Roman civil service. This fact is suggested by the dedication to a man named Theophilus, who is addressed in a manner that suggests he was a Roman official. In specific, Theophilus is referred to as "most excellent" (in Greek "kratiste), a title typically used when addressing important officials. On three other occasions, for example, Luke used the term "kratiste" to refer to Roman officials (*Luke* 23:26, 24: 3, and 26:25.) It seems reasonable to assume that his use of the term in his dedication (Luke 1:3) also indicated that Theophilus is an official.

Arguing this case, for example, Barclay (1975) observes "The book was written to a man called Theophilus. He is called 'most excellent Theophilus' and the title given him is the normal title for a high official in the Roman government."

Scholars also believe that Luke might have been cultivating this civil servant in order to sway Roman officials to abandon their anti-Christian actions. Thus Danker (1988 25), theorizes "To judge from the honorific "most excellent" (*kratiste*), Theophilos (Latin, Theophilus) appears to be a Roman official with a Greek name who might do much to clear the Christians of anti-Roman activity."

This chain of thought is continued by Maddox (1982 13) who affirms that: "Theophilus is a magistrate of some kind, and he and his colleagues have received unfavorable reports, about Christianity....Luke writes to correct the misinformation, i.e. his work is an apology for Christianity [aimed at Roman civil servants.]"

Generalizing his depiction of Theophilus, Bruce observes (1998 29)

> It is quite probable that Theophilus was a representative member of the intelligent middle-class public at Rome whom Luke wished to win over to a less prejudiced and more favorable opinion of Christianity than that which was current among them....Theophilus had already learned something about the rise and progress of Christianity, and Luke's aim was to put him in possession of more accurate information than he already had.

Luke, furthermore, had reason to curry the favor of Roman civil servants. In the recent past, Nero had severely persecuted Christians and the memory of such horrific treatment, no doubt, lingered in the minds of many Christians. Claudius (the emperor after Caligula), furthermore, installed Herod Agrippa as the king of Galilee, Judea, and Peraea. Herod was known to persecute Christians. Luke probably wrote in a period when a lull in the attacks on Christianity existed, but when a resumption of such hostile action was clearly a possibility (as history bears out.) This lowering of hostilities apparently gave Luke a window of opportunity where he could receive a relatively fair hearing from members of the Roman civil service. Luke wrote his account of Christianity to a Roman civil servant as an apology for the faith at exactly this moment in time.

The Stoic Bias of Roman Officials

Stoicism tended to be the philosophical foundation of the Roman civil service while other powerful forces within the empire favored Epicureanism. Because stoicism provided the prevailing moral code for the Roman civil service, those in politics tended to embrace it. Thus "Epicureanism tended to be favored in the ranks in Rome's military, while stoicism appealed to members of the Senate and other political movers and shakers. Many Roman politicians at least adopted the high moral tone of Stoicism according to which only virtue is a genuine good, while money, health, and even life itself are simply preferred indifferents" (Stanford 16.)

A key aspect of stoicism is the idea of "natural law." This perspective argues that the laws of mankind should be based on the laws of nature. Modern legal codes still have elements of natural law (although considerable debate rages regarding what is "natural.") Thus, it is permissible to kill someone who is attempting to kill you, because doing so is a natural response. The stoics believed that all people were subject to a universal nature and they that inevitably respond accordingly. This belief had an important impact upon Roman law. Thus, "Roman jurists adapted some of the Stoic ideas of natural law in their expositions of the civil law" (Brown, Beverly and Neil McCormick (1998 12.)

Cicero, the great Roman writer and orator provides a classic overview of the stoic view of natural law:

> True law is right reason in agreement with Nature....it is of universal application, unchanging and everlasting...we need not look outside ourselves for an....interpreter of it. And there will not be different laws at Rome and at Athens or different laws now and in the future, but one eternal and unchangeable law will be valid for all nations and for all times...Whoever is disobedient is fleeing from himself and denying his human nature and by this very fact he will suffer the worst penalties, even if he escapes what is commonly considered punishment.(Cicero (1928.)

Two famous stoics whose works were readily available and much respected when Luke wrote include Cicero (106-43 BC), a great orator and champion of the Roman republic and Virgil (70-19 BC) whose *Aeneid* is a stoic classic that affirmed in compelling ways that Rome was fated for greatness and goodness. Virgil's stoic poetry combined a love for Rome with Stoic principles in ways that inspired the Roman civil service.

One only has to look at the character of Aeneas in the *Aeneid* to see how stoic principles were infused in this great epic of the founding of Rome:

> As in many other epics, Aeneas, the hero, is depicted as a character who embodies traits the audience values, respects, and cherishes. [In ways that reflect stoic dictates] Aeneas "accepts his destiny of helping to found a great nation (that inevitably evolves into the Roman Empire) and he constantly

puts the needs of Rome above his own desires... Like the American cowboy hero, Aeneas is a bigger-than-life hero who disregards his own needs in order to advance the cause of his nation." (Walle 2001 6.)

This pro-stoic theme in the *Aeneid* is hardly an accident. Virgil was best friends with Emperor Augustus who commissioned Virgil to write the work in a way that would provide an apology for the new government of Rome that was becoming increasingly centralized. Virgil did so by merging legend, myth, and a stoic theme that portrayed Rome following an inevitable mission to towards greatness (Walle 2001.) As Walle observes:

> The *Aeneid* both underscores the destiny of Rome (to become an empire) and urges all Romans to follow Aeneas's example and make personal sacrifices to help Rome achieve its destiny. Thus, the *Aeneid* most basically is an outstanding piece of promotional literature for legitimatization of the Roman Empire. The broad strategy of the project was suggested by the emperor himself, and the piece was written by the emperor's best friend.

Roman officials were greatly influenced by such logic and largely embraced a stoic perspective of the world, viewing Rome as the fulfillment of a glorious and beneficial destiny. Thus, the powerful civil servants of the era tended to view the Roman Empire (and their work as agents of it) from a stoic perspective.

These same officials looked with a jaundice eye upon their Epicurean rivals. Instead of envisioning the destiny of Rome, the nobleness of sacrifice, and the legitimacy of natural law, Epicureans were concerned with their own pleasure, retiring from the world to reduce stress and pain in order to focus upon their personal pleasure, not some greater good. While, in actuality, the Epicurean philosophy was sophisticated and emphasized moderation, detractors stereotyped it as hedonistic to a fault and unconcerned with anything but physical pleasures. This negative stereotype is juxtaposed with the stoics' willingness to suffer (as Aeneas did) in order to advance the collective good, and support Rome.

Luke's Anti-Epicurean Posture

Luke's "Rich Fool" reflects the same anti-Epicurean bias that was prevalent in stoicism the attitudes of the Roman civil service.) *Luke's* "Rich Fool" has no regard for anything except a hedonistic lifestyle. Such a depiction reflects common stereotypes of Epicureanism that were despised by the stoics and represent the antithesis of the stoic way of life. Stoics would have approved of

Luke's version, where the soul of a "fool" is taken before he can enjoy his hedonistic frenzy. This suffering to come would have been a surprise to the Epicurean "fool" who did not believe in an afterlife or that the gods intervened in human affairs.

The parable makes an illusion to a well-known cliché used to negatively depict the Epicurean perspective: "Eat, drink and be merry for tomorrow you may die." (12: 19.) Luke is hardly being subtle here and his message would have been understood by the stoic civil servants he was addressing.

Scholarship on the parable of the "Rich Fool", however, does not make this connection; thus, Hultgren states "The final saying ("eat, drink, and be merry) is commonplace. Similar sayings appear elsewhere in Jewish Tradition (LXX Exxl 8: 15 having the same Greek verbs as here.") Various other commentators focus upon *Old Testament* precedents and ignore Epicurean parallels.

While the Epicureans believed that there is no afterlife and that the soul perished after the physical death of the body, *Luke*'s "Rich Fool" learns his soul is demanded by God. This reflects a stoic vision that people are part of a larger and eternal universe and that those who contribute to it will ultimately merge with nature (in some vague manner) and those who don't will suffer.

Luke transformed the plotline of the "Rich Fool" in order to emphasize these key points. In the *Thomas* version, apparently written before *Luke* or based on a version that predates *Luke*), the "Rich Fool" is depicted as an investor who is hoping to maximize his profits instead of being a consumer seeking to enjoy his wealth by eating drinking and being merry. In this regard Luddemann observes "This exemplary narrative [of *Thomas*] is related to *Luke* 12: 16–20. But the economic circumstances are slightly different. In *Luke* we have a farmer who want to 'save', here [in *Thomas*] a businessman who wants to put his money to work." (2000 621.)

Thus, the portrayal in *Thomas* does not deal with an Epicurean theme; *Thomas*' "Rich Fool", in contrast, is depicted as a strategic individual and no discussion of any hedonistic tendencies are to be found. *Luke*'s "Rich Fool", in contrast, is overtly and explicitly interested in using his wealth to enjoy life and there is no discussion of shrewdness or a calculation of future profits. Thus, *Luke*'s "Rich Fool" reflects negative stereotypes of Epicureanism while *Thomas*' does not. The adjusted version found in *Luke* would have impressed Roman officials (who were pro-business, but anti-Epicurean.)

Christian traditions, furthermore, emphasize that people, once converted to Christianity, are "born again." While this phrase does not refer to a second physical birth (as New *Testament* passages indicate), it is still useful to compare this belief to what Epirurus had to say:

We are born once and cannot be born twice, but for all time must be no more. But you who are not master of to-morrow, postpone your happiness; life is wasted on procrastination and each one of us dies without allowing himself leisure.(Oates 1940 40.)

In both the *Luke* and *Thomas* versions, the "Parable of the Rich Fool", most generally, concerns stewardship. The stoics were equally interested in stewardship that was concerned with the general good. Such actions tended to be the model of the Roman civil service. Drawing parallels between Christian and stoic attitudes towards stewardship would be another way for Luke to emphasize to the Roman civil service that Christianity paralleled stoicism in important ways and was not a threat to Rome.

From Neutral to Partisan

Thus, the "Parable of the Rich Fool", as it is presented in *Luke*, appears to be a partisan jab at a particular philosophy that was opposed by both stoics and Christians. An old Middle Eastern proverb goes "The enemy of my enemy is my friend." Luke seems to have been using such logic in a ploy designed to help Christians to win more favorable treatment from Rome. Thus, if both stoics and Christians are enemies of the Epicureans, this would make Christians and the Roman civil service (largely stoics) allies and friends.

In order to make this case, Luke apparently took a parable that had previously been used to express a generic message about stewardship and greed and recast it in order to specifically critique Epicureans. Doing so portrayed stoics and Christians as having one mind in their mutual rejection of the Epicurean system.

In Table 4.3 we find:

Table 4.3: Motifs in *Luke*'s The "Rich Fool"

Motif	Description	Analysis
Great Success	Protagonist receives great return that is more than can be used or stored.	The protagonist is in a position to share his bounty, consume it in search of pleasure, or use it to generate future profits.
Hedonistic decision	The decision is made to hoard the riches so it can be used to generate future pleasure.	The goal of the individual is Epicurean and is stated in ways that reflect prevailing stereotypes of the Epicureans.
Anticipates future	The man believes he has many years to enjoy his wealth	Stoics encouraged people not to project the future, but to take life the way it comes and adjust accordingly
God intercedes	God calls the man a "fool" and takes action against him	Epicureans believed the gods are not involved in human affairs. The "Rich Fool" learns otherwise
An afterlife exists	God takes the man's soul.	Epicureans do not believe in an afterlife, and *Luke*'s "Rich Fool" learns otherwise, because God takes his soul.
No predicting	God asks the man what will happen to his riches now that his soul has been taken.	Stoics were taught to be indifferent to wealth and other comforts and focus on being noble. The Epicurean "Rich Fool" learns this would have been a good strategy.
Discussion	In *Thomas*, the parable appears to be a generic morality tale about greed and stewardship, not reflective of Epicureanism in any specific way. In *Luke*, in contrast, a strong Epicurean theme is developed. This motif would have been very meaningful to members of the Roman civil service allowing Luke to portray Christianity in a positive way that encouraged better treatment for the church.	

So viewed, the case is made that Luke consciously edited material he had available in order to impress his target audience in partisan ways. This analysis implies that Luke reworked the parable in redactive ways in order to achieve a conscious goal.

Conclusion

The "Parable of the Rich Fool" (variants of which exist in the *Gospel of Thomas* and the *Gospel of Luke*) has been examined. Although some scholars dismiss the differences between the two versions as superficial and not significant, that theory is challenged here.

This paper argues that Luke transformed a generic parable about stewardship and greed in order to make a rather pointed repudiation of Epicurean philosophy. Luke's reason for doing so was to impress the Roman civil service who tended to be stoics (rivals of Epicureanism.) By doing so, Luke hoped to win more favorable treatment for Christians when they dealt with Roman officials. Thus, the changes found in *Luke's* version of the "parable of the Rich Fool" do not seem to be random and superficial. Instead, they indicate conscious and calculated redactive editing that was accomplished in order to help Luke achieve his goal: favorably impressing the Roman civil service.

References

W. Barclay, (1975) *Luke, Daily Study Bible Series, revised edition,* (Philadelphia, Pennsylvania,),

Beavis, Mary Ann (1997) "The Foolish Landowner (*Luke* 12:16b–20)" in *Jesus and His Parables: Interpreting the Parables of Jesus Today* edited by V. George Shillington (Edinburgh: T and T. Clark.)

Birdsall, J. Neville (1962) "Luke 12:16 and the Gospel of Thomas" *Journal of Theological Studies* 332-6

Blomberg, Criag L. (1990) *Interpreting the Parables* (Downers Grove, Illinois: Intervarsity Press.)

Brown, Beverly and Neil McCormick (1998) "Law (Philosophy of)" *Routledge Encyclopedia of Philisophy* [online.] (www.rep.routledge.com/aritcle 001#T0011P5.16) p. 12

Bruce, F. F. (1998) , "The Book of Acts," *The International Commentary on the New Testament"* revised edition. Edited by William Reuben Farmer. 1506-46.

Danker, F. W. (1988) *Jesus and the New Age, revised edition,* (Philadelphia.)

DeWitt, Norman Wentworth (1954) *St. Paul and Epicurus* (Minneapolis, Minnesota: University of Mennesota Press.)

Funk, Robert W. and Hoover Roy W. (1997) *The Five Gospels: What Did Jesus Really Say?* (New York: Harper Collins.)

Hultgren, Arland J. (2000) *The Parables of Jesus: A Commentary* (Grand Rapids: William B. Eerdman.)

Jeremian, Joachim (1963) *The Parables of Jesus* (New York: Charles Scribner's Sons.)

Jones, Peter Rhea (1999) *Studying the Parables of Jesus* (Macon, Georgia: Smyth and Helwys.)

Julicher, Adolph (1899) *Die Glrichnisreden Jesu* (J. C. B. Mohr.) Two Volumes.

Kirby, W. J. Torrance (2003) "Stoic and Epicurean? Calvin's Dialectical Account of Providence in the Institute" *International Journal of Systematic Theology* V. 5 # 3 pp 309-22.)

Lowery, Richard H. (1993) "Sabbath and Survival: Abundance and Self-Restraint in a Culture of Excess" *Encounter* 143-67.

Lundemann, Gerd (2001) *Jesus After 2000 Years* (New York: Prometheus)

Malherbe, Abraham J. (1999) "Anti-Epiurean Rhetoric in 1 Thessalonians" *Text und Geshichte* p. 136-42

Marxsen, Willi (1954) *Mark the Evangelist* (Nashville: Abingdon Press.)

Nichelsburg, George W. E. (1978-9) Riches, the Rich, and God's Judgment in 1 Enoch 92-105 and the Gospel According to Luke" *New Testament Studies* 25 324-32.

Oates, Whitney J. (1940) *The Stoic and Epicurean Philosophers: The Complete Extant Writings of Epiturus, Epictetus, Lucretius, and Marcus Aurelius* (New York: The Modern Library.)

Pagels, Elaine (2003) Beyond Belief (New York: Random House.)

Scott, Bernard Brandon (2002) *Re-imagine the World: An Introduction to the Parables of Jesus* (Santa Rosa, California: Polebridge Press)

(Stanford 2006) *The Encyclopedia of Philosophy* [online] (plato.stanford.edu/ entries/stoicism.)

Stanton, Graham (2002) *The Gospels and Jesus* (Oxford: Oxford University Press)

Tomlin, Graham (1997) "Christians and Epicureans in *1 Corinthians*" *Journal of Studies in the New Testament* V. 68 p. 51-72

Walle, Alf H. (2001) "The Positioning of Good News" in *Rethinking Marketing: Qualitative Strategies and Exotic Visions* (Westport, Connecticut: Quorum Books.)

Whenham, David (1989) *The Parables of Jesus* (Downers Grove, Illinois: Intervarsity.)

White, James R. (1998) "The Jesus Seminar and the Gospel of Thomas: Courting the Media at the Cost of Truth" *Christian Research Journal* V 20 January-March 51-2.

Wright, Stephen I. (2000) "Parables on Poverty and Riches (Luke 12:13-21; 16:1-13; 16:19-31" in *The Challenges of Jesus' Parables* Edited by Richard M. Longenecker (Grand Rapids William B. Eerdmans) pp 217-39.

Chapter 5

Christianity, Bacchus, and Sexual License:

Introduction

The *Epistle of Jude* is often dismissed as a short *New Testament* letter that deals in generic ways with false teachings. Arguing this position, Brown asserts "most people find this brief work too negative, too dated, and too apocalyptic to be of much use" (1997 748.) Harris, emphasizing the general tone observes that the author of *Jude* does not "specify his opponent's doctrinal errors or refute their arguments" (2002 385.) Connick's (1978 374) views are representative of those who suggest that *Jude* is written to a broad audience and that its theme is very general; he observes "The salutation fits any Greek-speaking community...the author's message is appropriate for any and all churches threatened by unacceptable and immoral practices that are condemned." Probably because of this relatively low opinion within the scholarly community, Rowston has described the *Epistle of Jude* as "the most ignored book in the *New Testament*" (1975 554.)   An impressive review of the literature that ranges from ancient times to the present is provided by Kenneth Lyle (1998 37–68.)

Lyle, a specialist with a sophisticated view of the epistle, argues that *Jude* deserves increased attention because it deals with the early church and the environment in which it existed (1998.) Further evidence regarding the importance of The Epistle of *Jude* is the praise it received from Origen in his *Commentary on Matthew* who observed that *Jude* was "packed with sound words of heavenly grace." Such an evaluation seems to indicate that *Jude* is more than merely a generic and pedestrian encouragement to the faithful; this praise is evidence that in its time *Jude* uniquely dealt with an issue of vital importance to the early church. Modern scholars, however, have been unable to adequately identify this significant content.

This analysis agrees with Lyle's basic premise that *The Epistle of Jude* provides important evidence regarding how the infant church responded and evolved during its early era. The epistle was written sometime before 120 AD and possibly much earlier (Hartington 2003 183.) During that era, all Christians would have been united by some kind of belief in Christ, but the religion had not yet solidified any well defined and universally accepted doctrine. Its author wrote in a time of confusion and false teachers. Other references to heretical influences, of course, are found in the writings of Paul, Peter, etc. as well as in the *Epistle of Jude*; collectively, they demonstrate that considerable polemics existed within the early church. Although, with hindsight, scholars might be able to discern the Christian tradition that ultimately emerged and, in teleological fashion, envision how the church developed; those who lived, believed, and worshipped during those early days would have only seen factions, disagreements, and rival beliefs that needed to be addressed on a case by case basis.

When describing the false teachers that threatened the church, Biblical scholars often point to the Judiazers and/or the Gnostics. Harrington, for example, observes:

> In the interpretation of *Jude* it has often been customary to link the intruders to some early from of Gnosticism. But this approach involved explaining one unknown by another unknown, since the origin and character of early Gnosticism are matters of great dispute and unclarity (2003 181.)

Linking Jude's opponents with Gnosticism, however, is difficult because the heretics attacked in the *Epistle of Jude* were apparently interested in ritualistic sexual intercourse while the Gnostics were indifferent to issues and pleasures of the flesh. Although some Gnostics felt free to engage in sexual activity in the belief that doing so was a meaningless diversion that would not undercut their soul, rituals that raised intercourse to a sacred level would not have made sense to them.

Harrington continues by pointing out that others simply throw up their hands in despair and lament that the text does not reveal any meaningful information about the author's opponents. He states:

> "Another approach is to give up on the problem of the intruders' identity by saying that their precise character is beyond understanding because Jude's language is too general and stereotyped to allow any real insight into the group he was attacking" (2003 181.)

This doubt raises an important questions. Did the Judiazers and the Gnostics provide the only rival perspectives of significance that existed within the early church? To what extent do the polemics mentioned in the *New Testament* stem from Pagan beliefs and their traditions? How does *Jude* fit into such controversies?

This essay deals with these issues by suggesting that the author of *Jude* wrote with specific ideas and opponents in mind. Indeed, a close reading of this short document suggests that it was opposing inroads that had been made by followers of the cult of Bacchus/Dionysus (Dionysus being the Greek version of Bacchus) who were attempting to infiltrate the church. As such, the *Epistle of Jude* demonstrates that the early church existed within the context of the mystery religion tradition and that the espstle actively opposed merging Christianity with this specific cult.

The Gentile Connection

As is universally accepted by *Biblical* scholars, the early church (following Paul's lead) actively reached out to the gentile world. Gentile converts to Christianity, no doubt, brought elements of their heritage and pre-existing beliefs with them when they joined. This would have been more prevalent in ancient times than today because Roman gentiles often worshipped a number of gods and they did not feel the need to reject other gods when accepting new ones. Just the opposite; according to the principle of syncretism, attempts were made to equate the gods of different people in the belief that universal gods had been independently discovered and worshipped by the members of various cultures.

To what extent did these early gentile converts attempt to reconcile their earlier religious heritage with Christianity? Were the dissenters that *Jude* discredits attempting to merge the old with the new into some kind of spiritual hybrid? Could such tendencies have changed the complexion of some congregations and/or triggered internal strife and debate?

A study of religious evolution reveals that vestigial remains of an earlier spiritual system often survive after people are converted to a new religion. If this is true, the early church may have risked being molded by the previous religious heritage of newly converted members.

The present author's work with Native Alaskans provides many examples of people who are loyal Christians and yet preserve a large part of their pre-contact cultural legacy and spiritual heritage. These Native Alaskans, furthermore, are approximately 100 years away from their pre-Christian era (a much longer time than that of recently converted gentile Christians of the 1st century.) These Native Alaskan converts, furthermore, lived in a world where their culture and heritage has largely been overpowered by a dominant outside traditions that have been forced upon them. Early gentile Christians who (1) only recently converted to a weak and evolving Christianity and (2) who lived in a world where their the pre-Christian cultural and religious heritage continued to dominate would probably exhibit remnants of their traditional heritage to an even larger degree.

Thus, in all likelihood these gentile converts would not be prone to completely abandon their earlier life and worldview. That, in the final analysis, is the way in which cultural and religious change typically takes place within a strong and dominant culture that is not overtly threatened. Since gentile converts undoubtedly brought aspects of their previous cultural and religious heritage to the church, scholars need to consider how this preexisting thinking, habits, and beliefs changed Christianity or threatened to do so.

Clues in the *New Testament* indicate that recent converts continued to embrace their old ways at least to a degree. In *1 Corinthians* (8:11–3), for example, Paul notes that some members of the church were prone to stumble back towards Paganism and that care needed to be taken to prevent such defections. This is dramatized when Paul encourages people to refrain from eating meat that has been sacrificed (an acceptable practice for Christians) if doing so might help prevent recently converted gentile Christians from backsliding to their Pagan heritage.

Thus, Paul overtly acknowledges that many members of the early church continued to be influenced by Paganism and he laments that they could easily return to their old religion. Overtly or covertly, these gentile Christians continued to harbor Pagan tendencies. Could some of these converts have attempted to merge Christianity with aspects of their earlier religions? And, if so, could such attempts have resulted in conflict within the church?

Ultimately, of course, much of the ceremonial life of the Christian religion has some sort of Pagan connection or precedent. Well known examples include the fact that Christ's birthday came to be associated with the birthday of Mithras (the sun god) even though Christ was not born at this time of the year. The celebration of Easter, furthermore, is linked to fertility symbols because it came to be associated with a celebration of the returning of life that occurs every spring. Many ancient Gods, furthermore, were ultimately recast as saints (and/or the holidays of these gods were replaced by Christian celebrations), etc. When the Pagan traditions were still strong in the minds of recent converts wouldn't a tendency exist for elements of Paganism to merge with the fluid and evolving Christianity that existed at that time?

The Mystery Religion Tradition

Gentile Christianity emerged in a world where many "mystery religions" already existed. These Pagan organizations provided comfort, companionship, and the promise of eternal life. Christianity, at least outwardly, shared many elements with the mystery religions.

Wilken (2003 44–7) goes to great lengths to show how Christianity had an outward appearance of being just another secret association or mystery religion. He quotes liberally from early Christian apologist Tertullian who explains Christianity in terms of the tradition of Roman associations. Wilken seems to suggest that Tertullian presents the church in this way as a tactic of argumentation. A question remains, however: to what degree did early Christianity actually function as a mystery religion and/or as a Roman association? Is Tertullian merely reporting the facts when he describes Christianity? Perhaps his words should be taken as face value.

No doubt Christianity was perceived to be a mystery religion by the gentiles who came into contact with it. Even without the documentation that Wilken provides, common sense tells us this would have been the case. Perhaps (if not probably) various converts joined the church in the belief that it was another mystery religion. New converts, furthermore, probably did not completely abandon their belief in synchronism immediately upon conversion. They were not expected to do so when they joined other sects.

Could some of the "false teachers" mentioned within the New Testament be gentile Christians who sought to blend or merge elements of the pre-existing mystery religions with an evolving Christianity that had not yet developed a definite or formal structure? If so, are some of the false teachers mentioned in the *New Testament* gentile converts or envoys from Pagan cults, not Judiazers and/or Gnostics? This analysis addresses this issue though an examination of *Jude*.

The Cult of Bacchus: An Overview

Various commentators draw linkages between Christianity and the Pagan deities. Wilken, for example, mentions the theory that Christianity paralleled the cult of Bacchus (a fertility god) in various ways. In ancient times did connections exist between Christianity and the worship of Bacchus? Wilken does not rule this out.

As will be dealt with in more detail below, significant parallels between the worship of Bacchus and Christianity are obvious and overt. Christ's first miracle, for example, involved turning water into wine. Wine, of course, was central to the cult of Bacchus. Being a fertility god, springtime was a favorite time of worship for devotees of Bacchus/Dionysus. The Christian Easter also takes place in the spring and has been linked to fertility (eggs and prolifically reproducing bunnies, for example, are symbols of fertility that continue to be identified with Easter.) Both Jesus and Bacchus offer a resurrection.

Bacchus was a Middle Eastern God that had been worshipped within the West long enough to become accepted within the ancient pantheon of Greece and Rome. He was a god of fertility. Thus, Long (2003 753) has observed, "The phallic procession was a typical form of the rites of Dionysus and was intended to promote fertility."

The worship of Bacchus involved mind altering orgies (drinking bouts), the aforementioned phallic procession, and (according to some reports) ritualistic sexual activity. Unfortunately for the cult, the carnal excesses of festivals honoring Bacchus eventually prompted the Roman Government to suppress the religion and its form of worship.

Wilken believes that in the minds of Pagans, Christianity could have been mistaken for (or lumped with) groups such as the cult of Bacchus. Was doing so merely a case of mistaken identity? Or, in contrast, did the early church, members of it, or envoys to it embrace elements of the cult of Bacchus? Could the reports of a connection between Bacchus and Christianity be based upon actual observation?

The *Epistle of Jude* condemns a group of Christians (or possibly pseudo or heretical Christians) who infiltrate a congregation and apparently encourage the members to engage in some sort of sexual behavior within the context of Christian ritual. Could these interlopers be members of a hybrid group of Christians who sought to combine the worship of Bacchus and Jesus? If this had been the case, the arguments put forth in the *Epistle of Jude* letter would have been exactly the same as they now exist.

Ritualistic Versus Recreational Sex

There has been a tendency to explain references to sinful carnal behavior mentioned in the epistles by pointing to the presumed moral slackness of the age. Thus, Corinth is routinely described a seaport full of lustful single men out for a good time. Such uncouth traveling men and their habits, however, would not have been much of a threat to the church; after all, they are ubiquitous in all cultures including our own, but they have not destroyed organized religion. Pious and religious converts continuing to engage in ritualized sexual behavior associated with the Pagan gods, in contrast, would be a much greater threat to the church than the erotic dallying of drunken sailors.

This raises an important question: might some of the condemnations of sexual behavior in the *New Testament* refer to ritualistic intercourse that took place within the context of Pagan worship? If gentile converts continued to interact with various mystery religions (possibly within the context of ritualistic intercourse), they would have failed to become truly and completely Christian. This would constitute a major threat to the church.

Paul encourages people to exercise restraint in their sexual lives. Scholars have often interpreted these suggestions in purely moralistic terms and/or assumed that Paul merely wanted people to remain focused on Godly issues, not the pleasures of the flesh. In addition, however, strict controls on sexual behavior would indirectly outlaw ritualistic sexual activities associated with the Pagan Gods. Could Paul's strict teachings on sexual behavior be a covert way to encourage newly converted believers to sever all ties with their Pagan heritage including ritualistic intercourse? Such a theory is bolstered by Paul's concern (discussed above) that newly converted Christians are prone to backsliding and need to be protected from temptation. The church obviously needed a strong arsenal of controls to prevent such lapses.

This analysis argues that the *Epistle of Jude* is an attack upon those who had leanings towards the cult of Bacchus. Such a theory focuses upon significant elements of the epistle that have not been adequately explicated. A key emphasis of this argument is that the early church feared Pagan false teachers in addition to Judiazers and Gnostics.

Jude and Bacchus: The Evidence

The author of the *Epistle of Jude* expresses concern because devotees to Bacchus were encouraging the church (or some of its members) to embrace their cult in some form or manner. By looking at (1) the text of the *Epistle of Jude*, (2) the situation of the ancient church, and (3) the Roman repression experienced by the cult of Bacchus, the message of *Jude* can be more effectively reconstructed. When viewed in this manner, the epistle emerges as much more than a generic criticism of immorality, fornication, etc.

In arguing this point, evidence will be presented regarding (1) the benefits that the cult of Bacchus would have received by merging with or infiltrating Christianity, (2) similarities between the cult of Bacchus and Christianity, (3) the ancient tendency towards syncretism (4) the sexual nature of the false teachings that the author of *Jude* opposed, (5) Jewish/Christian prohibitions against earthy women mating with supernatural creatures, (6) the fact that the cult of Bacchus involves earthly women mating with supernatural creatures, and (7) the symbolism of the goat. Each will be discussed separately.

A Motive for the Cult of Bacchus

The cult of Bacchus had much to gain by becoming involved with early Christianity. Doing so might have eased the restrictions on the cult imposed by the Roman government and, thereby, the position of Bacchus within the religions of the Roman world would have been enhanced.

Although the cult of Bacchus was an important religion, the Roman government had placed tight controls on the way in which worship could be conducted. Although handicapped by these restrictions, the cult continued to exist.

While some of the original patterns of devotion may have involved only women, festivals were gradually expanded to include men as well, "...men were allowed to take part and these [festivals] may have been characterized by sexual freedom" (De Houghton 1985 587.)

As time went on, governmental restrictions limiting the free and unhindered worship of Bacchus arose. The reason for the restrictions was related to the fact that the festivals tended to degenerate in to drunken, sexual orgies:

> These events [their festivals], which supposedly originated in spring nature festivals, became occasions for licentiousness and intoxication, at which the celebrants danced, drank, and generally debauched themselves. The Bacchanalia became more and more extreme and were prohibited by the Roman Senate in 186 BC. In the first century AD, however, the Dionysiac [Dionysus is Greek form of Bacchus] mysteries were still popular (Funk and Wagnall 1995.)

Although legal restraints were imposed on the cult, it survived.

No doubt, devotees of Bacchus living in the early Christian era wanted to reestablish a greater freedom of worship and, in general, strengthen the position of the religion. In the early days, the Romans viewed Christianity as a branch of Judaism, a religion that was sanctioned by Rome. If the cult of Bacchus, long discriminated against by the Roman government, could become identified with or merged with Christianity (initially viewed as a sect of Judaism a favored religion that had been granted relative freedom of worship), the cult could, in effect, receive a new "charter" and, thereby, gain a greater degree of religious freedom. Thus, a clear motive for devotees of Bacchus to identify and equate their God with Jesus existed.

Similarity between the cult of Bacchus and Christianity

If devotees of Bacchus had wanted to become involved with Christianity, similarities between the two (even if only superficial) were needed to justify such a merging. If there were absolutely no parallels between the two, the rationale for forging some kind of an alliance would have been implausible.

In point of fact, however, Bacchus shares important similarities with Jesus that could have provided a rationale for merging of the two Gods. Although these similarities seem to be coincidental and do not appear to be the result of cultural diffusion (or stem from any common origin), parallels exist, nonetheless. Thus:

> Like Jesus, Dionysus is a God in human form, who dies and is resurrected, born of a mortal mother by a divine father. Like Jesus, Dionysus is a god whose tragic passion is re-enacted by eating his flesh and drinking his blood. Like Jesus, Dionysus is a miraculous god associated with the immortality of the soul. Like Christianity, the religion of Dionysus spread like wildfire. (from *Treading the Winepress* part 2)

These issues and parallels will be discussed individually.

Both Bacchus and Christ die and are resurrected

Christianity, of course, accepts Jesus as the son of God. Jesus chooses to die to save people from their sins. After being killed in a shameful and degrading manner, Jesus is resurrected from the dead. By accepting his fate, Jesus provides sinful people with a means of salvation and a chance for resurrection and eternal life. Jesus' example facilitates people overcoming their sins and shows that they can receive the benefits of an eternal life.

Bacchus is a fertility god. In harmony with the seasons of the year (in which plants grow to maturity and die, only to return to life in the spring) Bacchus dies in the fall and is resurrected in the spring. As Long has observed., "In Asia Minor the rites were generally held in spring and were based on the belief that Dionysus, as a vegetation god, died in winter and was reborn in the spring" (2003 753.) People came to believe that Bacchus held the keys to resurrection and that individual people could gain assess to eternal life by belief, ritual, and worship.

The rationale for immortality presented in the cult of Bacchus, of course, is very different from the Christian belief that Jesus died for the sins of mankind and offered eternal life within this context. Viewed very broadly, however, both Jesus and Bacchus experience a personal resurrection and offer eternal life to believers. As a result of this similarity, devotees of Bacchus would, at least initially, feel a connection to Jesus and Christianity and vice versa. Devotees of Bacchus would also have had a "bargaining chip" to use in negotiations with Christians because they could point to this parallel.

Jesus and Bacchus are born of a divine father and earthly mother

Christ is the only son of the only God who is born of Mary, an earthly woman. Dionysus'/Bacchus' father is Zeus (the king of the Gods) and Semele, an earthly woman. As with the parallels involving eternal life, similarities between the parents of Christ and Bacchus appear to be merely coincidental, not the product of cultural diffusion or borrowings. Nonetheless, Bacchus and Christ both have a divine father and a mortal mother. This similarity that would have been crucial to devotees of Bacchus as well as providing additional reasons to justify a merger between the cult and the church.

Blood and flesh of both Gods were ritualistically consumed

Christians ritualistically eat the flesh of Christ and drink his blood. This ceremony is performed in remembrance of Christ's statements at the last supper and his sacrifice on the behalf of an undeserving mankind.

As festivals honoring Bacchus, worshippers also ceremonially eat the flesh of the god and drink his blood. Apparently this practice was inspired by a legend regarding Bacchus in which "Dionysus was seized by the Titans, who tore him limb from limb and began to cook him up for a meal [but he was] restored to life by Rhea (his earth goddess Grandmother" (De Houghton 19985 586.)

Eventually this bit of lore came to be reenacted within festivals and worship involving Bacchus. Thus, De Houghton observes:

> In the Dionysus cult, the rending and devouring of raw flesh is probably based in straightforward magic: you may become god by devouring god in one of his manifestations. The concept is not so far removed from that of the Christian who receives the wafer of consecrated bread during Holy Communion. (586.)

This ritual had a long history and it was not easily stamped out easily. Buckhardt, writing of the age of Constantine (centuries after *Jude* was written), for example, observes: "The mysteries of Bacchus...were still widely represented... [scholars] know they still involved devouring the raw and bloody flesh of a kid [young goat.]" 1949 (168) Such behavior, very much ingrained in the worship of Bacchus, was probably even more prominent before the twilight of the Pagan era when *Jude* was written.

The modern classicist Barry Powell (2001) goes so far as to argue that the Christian tradition of eating and drinking "the flesh" and "blood" of Jesus was influenced by the example of Dionysus. I doubt this is true because of the many other differences in the beliefs and rituals involving the two Gods. Nonetheless, inadvertent parallels between the ritualistic cannibalism of the cult of Bacchus and the Eucharist undoubtedly exist. These similarities could have suggested to devotees of Bacchus that a merging the two gods was feasible and appropriate.

Both Gods offer immortality

On many occasions, fertility gods and goddesses became associated in some manner with a belief in immortality. This connection is suggested by the fact that every year the world and its plants die with the coming of winter, but return to life in the spring. Bacchus is a fertility god that follows this pattern and devotees believed that he offered the hope of eternal life. The various ceremonies and festivals associated with Bacchus were hinged upon the concept of resurrection.

Jesus also offers resurrection and eternal life. Christ, of course, is not a fertility God and his means of providing eternal life are very different from metaphorically replicating the flowing of the seasons from winter (death) to spring (rebirth.) Nonetheless, both Christ and Bacchus die and return from the dead. In the process, both offer eternal life to believers.

The Christian ceremony of resurrection (Easter), furthermore, takes place in the spring, just when the major festival honoring Bacchus traditionally occurred.) Not only does this similarity exist, some Christian were reported to have worshiped in ways that are clearly reminiscent of festivals that honored Bacchus. Wilken, for example, observes, "[various elements of Bacchus festivals] for instance, the mingling of males and females, the abandonment of modesty, the indiscriminate defilement of women-appear in reports about the Christians" (Wilken 2003 17.)

Are these reports merely sensationalist accounts and/or the product of misinformation? Or do they reflect an objective account of some Christian behavior during an early age?

The influence of syncretism

In the Roman world, of course, there was a strong tendency for people to engage in syncretism: equating and merging the deities of different people in the belief that they had been independently discovered and worshiped within different cultures. Thus, the Greek Dionysus and the Roman Bacchus had come to be viewed as being the same god and the cults honoring them had been merged. If devotees of Bacchus believed that people who worshipped Christ were independently worshipping Bacchus, a campaign to incorporate Christianity under its banner could easily have developed.

Thus, a natural and predictable response on the part of the cult of Bacchus would be to send envoys to Christian congregations to encourage an alliance and/or a merging. These Pagans and their Christian advocates who wanted to apply the principle of syncretism to Christianity would have been dismissed as false teachers whose festivals and beliefs did not fit in with or reflect Christian traditions and dogma. Due to their sexual rituals and synergetic orientation, these Pagans would have been described as licentious false teachers who denied the unique divinity of Christ. This is the exact way in which they are portrayed in *Jude*.

Jude's View of the False Teachings

In various places throughout the *Bible*, reference is made to false teachers who were somehow associated with the Pagan gods. The most notable, perhaps, is Jezebel, a devotee of Baal. Ultimately, of course, the name and image of Jezebel came to be identified with those who sought to lure Christians to the worship of idols and Pagan gods. In the *Revelation*, furthermore, the Nicolatians are accused of encouraging fornication and eating sacrifices made to false idols (*Revelation* 2: 14.) In tandem with these complaints, *Jude* finds fault with those who (1) act in a sexually provocative manner during worship and (2) deny the uniqueness of Jesus. The overt description of such offenders is found in Verse 4 which states, "...ungodly men, turning the grace of our God into lasciviousness, and denying our only Master and Lord, Jesus Christ."

Devotees of Bacchus who (1) encouraged Christians to join in the sexually-oriented spring fertility rites and (2) argued that Christ was actually Bacchus would have appeared to the author of *Jude* in exactly this manner. Those who denied Christ's uniqueness while advocating ritualistic sexual intercourse would have been written off as lewd individuals who denied the divinity of Christ.

According to Harrington (2003 190) the Greek wording in *Jude* implies that the false teachers had been members of the church and, in their minds, were still a part of the congregation. In arguing against these men, the author of *Jude* invokes the sacred writings of Judaism in ways that counter the logic of synchronizers who sought to merge Christ and Bacchus. Thus, the seventh verse of the *Epistle of Jude* states: "Even as Sodom and Gomorrah, and the cities about them, having in like manner with these given themselves over to fornication and gone after strange flesh, are set forth as an example, suffering the punishment of eternal fire." In this context, "strange flesh" could refer to Gods/surrogate gods mating with earthly women in festivals honoring Bacchus.

The author of *Jude* is complaining about the dangers of ritualized sexual intercourse and dismissing it as fornication. The sexual behavior that occurred at festivals honoring Bacchus could easily have been interpreted in this manner and condemned accordingly.

Earthy Women and the Supernatural

In Verse 4 of *Jude*, the author observes that some members of the congregation are "ungodly men, turning the grace of our God into lasciviousness." While Harrington (2003 190) notes that such phraseology was often used to denote idolatry, he prefers a literal sexual interpretation; in the present analysis both meanings are viewed as appropriate because the false teachers encourage the worship of another God via ritualistic sexual intercourse. Harrington (2003 190) also observes that in ancient times (as today) people often attempt to undercut their rivals by depicting them as sexually immoral if the charge is legitimate or not. The reading presented in this analysis does not presuppose any kind of "smear campaign" by the author of the *Epistle of Jude* and accepts the charges of sexual behavior at face value.

In other words, the "false teachers" wanted to transform the Christian religion in ways that opponents would have viewed as lewd and lustful because they aroused and focused upon sexual desire. Having made this point, the author of *Jude* reminds the reader that God will punish those who encourage earthly women to mate with supernatural men. The author makes this argument by retelling an incident discussed in the sixth chapter of *Genesis* and the sixth chapter of *First Enoch* where angels come down and mate with earthly women. God is outraged by this offense and he places these sexually offending angels in "everlasting bonds under darkness until the judgment of the great day."

In other words, those who allow or encourage angels (supernatural beings) to mate with earthy women are likely to incur the wrath of God. In festivals honoring Bacchus, the god and/or his surrogates mate with earthly women:

> The worship of Dionysus or Bacchus took place every two years...when bacchantes took off to the mountains. Once beyond the reach of their men folk, they were inspired to ecstatic frenzy, drinking excessive amounts of wine and dancing wildly to the clashing of cymbals and the pounding of their long staffs. Dressed in flowing white, robes, their hair hanging loose and a deer skin draped around their shoulders, they whirled in the dance... (Anonymous.)

In addition:

> By the 5th century BC, Dionysus was also known to the Greeks as Bacchus, a name referring to the loud cries with which Dionysus was worshiped at the *orgia,* or Dionysiac mysteries. These frenetic celebrations, which probably originated in spring nature festivals, became occasions for licentiousness and intoxication. This was the form in which the worship of Dionysus became popular in the 2nd century BC in Roman Italy, where the Dionysiac mysteries were called the Bacchanalia. The indulgences of the Bacchanalia became increasingly extreme, and the celebrations were prohibited by the Roman Senate in 186 BC. In the 1st century AD, however, the Dionysiac mysteries were still popular, as evidenced by representations of them found on Greek sarcophagi. (Encarta 2005)

Eventually the rituals were expanded to several times a month and they became celebrations involving both sexes, not just women.

Thus, the rituals and festivals honoring Bacchus involve earthly women mating with a supernatural being and/or his surrogates. Doing so is exactly the type of behavior that the *Epistle of Jude* condemns and warns its readers about.

As discussed above, many Biblical scholars believe that the *Epistle of Jude* reveals very little about the false teachers who are being opposed. The author of *Jude*, in contrast, actually provides some specific details about his adversaries. These rivals advocate sexuality within the context of worship. This ritual is compared to the behavior of the fallen angels in *Genesis* and *First Enoch* who mated with earthly women. This description fits perfectly with devotees of the cult of Bacchus who might have been attempting to merge their cult with Christianity.

The Symbolism of the Goat

Thus far, this paper has made the case that the *Epistle of Jude* condemns ritualistic sexual intercourse involving earthly women and supernatural beings and that the author of *Jude* uses passages from the *Genesis* and *First Enoch* to bolster his case. Strong evidence, however, has not been presented that the author of the *Epistle of Jude* had the specific cult of Bacchus clearly in mind as the false teachers being discussed. After all, many mystery religions offered eternal life and ritualistic sexual intercourse was not limited to the cult of Bacchus.

A clue is provided, however, in the *First Enoch's* account of the angels mating with earthly women. *First Enoch* identifies the demon Azazel as the angel who leads his cohorts into mating with earthly women. Leaney (1967 89), for example, observes: "Azazel is one of the chief rebel angels [and] he seems to have been thought of as a demon living in the wilderness."

It is generally known that Azazel took the form of a goat. The word "scapegoat" derived from a story about him in the Old Testament. Eventually, of course, Satan came to be perceived as a goat.

Not only was Azazel portrayed as a goat, so was Bacchus. When at risk, Bacchus was transformed into a goat in order to disguise him from his enemies. As a young Child, Bacchus was in danger and he needed to hide his identity. "To protect the infant god, Hermes changed Dionysus into a baby goat and took him to a group of nymphs to be raised. While living in the mountains with the nymphs, Dionysus invented the process of growing grapes and making wine." (BBC.)

As a result, Bacchus has often been identified with the goat and portrayed as such "[artistic works often depict people] riding on the goat of lust or otherwise engaged in Bacchic rites. Depictions of satyrs and cloven-hoofed beasts setting upon innocent nymphs were extremely popular" (anonymous.) Using the symbolism of the goat to refer to Bacchus would have been obvious to the ancients to whom the *Epistle of Jude* was addressed.

Thus, the author of *Jude* points to an incident recorded in *Genesis* and *First Enoch* in which God becomes angry because a supernatural goat engages in sexual intercourse with earthly women. This incident is discussed with reference to complaints about licentious false teachers who the church must oppose. The association between (1) the goat and the supernatural beings that mate with earthly women and (2) the false teachers being criticized in *Jude* is close and direct. These parallels point to the possibility that the *Epistle of Jude* was a hostile critique of a faction of a Christian congregation that was connected in some way with Bacchus.

Thus, the author of *Jude* appears to embrace some rather pointed symbolism that directs attention towards devotees of the cult of Bacchus who wanted to merge with and/or transform the Christian church. The author of *Jude* uses Jewish texts to condemn this behavior in the strongest of ways.

Second Peter: A Reworking

Scholars have long seen a connection between the *Epistle of Jude* and *2 Peter*. The current opinion is that the author of *2 Peter* borrowed much material from the *Epistle of Jude*. Thus, *2 Peter* can be viewed as an adaptation of *Jude*'s original ideas that had been reworked in order to deal with the problems that existed when *2 Peter* was composed. The author of *2 Peter*, however, does not refer to or acknowledge the *Epistle of Jude*. As Harrington (2003 230) observes:

> in *2 Pet...*, the author makes abundant but selective use of *Jude* 6–18 as a source for terms and themes with which to denounce the "false teachers" he is opposing. However, he is not satisfied merely with copying from *Jude*. Rather, by strategic omissions, editorial changes, and additions he tailors his source to meet the threat posed by the opponents being confronted in this particular situation.

Under this sort of circumstance, scholars would expect the themes borrowed from the *Epistle of Jude* to be tailored for the specific occasion or circumstance for which they were used on a particular occasion.

In order to more efficiently deal with the message in *2 Peter*, its second chapter has been edited down for simplicity and clarity:

> 1. There arose false prophets...denying even the Master... 2....many shall follow their lascivious doings..., 10 [they are those] that walk after the flesh in the lust of defilement, and despise dominion. Daring, self-willed, they tremble not to rail at dignities: 14. having eyes full of adultery... [they] cannot cease from sin; enticing unsteadfast souls; 20. [Having] escaped the defilements of the world through the knowledge of the Lord and Savior Jesus Christ, they are again entangled therein and overcome [by their old ways.] 22. It has happened unto them according to the true proverb, The dog turning to his own vomit again, and the sow that had washed to wallowing in the mire.

The author of *2 Peter* is concerned because lascivious false prophets, who do not respect the legitimate leadership (despise dominion), entice the unsteadfast to reject the church and its teachings. While the author of *2 Peter* points to inappropriate sexual behavior, his major complaint seems to be that these false teachers reject Christianity because the second coming has not arrived in a timely manner. The author says the false teachers "come with mockery, walking after their own lusts, and saying, where is the promise of his coming?" (*2 Peter* 3 3–4.) These false teachers, furthermore, are depicted as members or former members of the church who had some stature and had won the respect of the congregation. Thus, *2 Peter* is not concerned with the threat of a rival mystery religion, but with the issue that some believers had lost faith because the second coming had not arrived and they were now encouraging others to follow their lead and reject the church.

This threat, of course, is a very different from the challenges presented by a rival Pagan religion attempting to usurp Jesus and/or manipulate Christianity for its own purposes. As a result, while much of the rhetoric of *2 Peter* is borrowed from the *Epistle of Jude*, strategic alterations deal with defections that arose when prophesies were not fulfilled in a timely manner.

Because the author of *2 Peter* is borrowing from the *Epistle of Jude* (and adapting it in ways that expand beyond the original context in which it was written, *2 Peter* is a more generic document that is preoccupied with internal scoffers and backsliders who reject the teachings of the church, not the evangelical efforts of another cult. As a result, pointed and specific references to an identifiable mystery religion have been edited out.

Conclusion

This essay points to evidence gained from a close reading of the *Epistle of Jude* that suggests the author was concerned because devotees of the cult of Bacchus were attempting to infiltrate and/or transform the church. A clear motive existed for the cult to move in that direction because the Roman government had put tight restrictions on the worship of Bacchus. By merging with a branch of Judaism (a religion favored by Rome), greater freedom for the cult could have resulted. Thus, devotees of Bacchus would have had much to gain from allying with the early Christians.

Various coincidental and inadvertent similarities between Christ and Bacchus provided the rationale to move in this direction. The rejection of the false teachers by the author of the *Epistle of Jude* is consistent with the theory that these heretics were allied with the cult of Bacchus. The author of *Jude*, for example, uses the example of supernatural beings mating with earthly women when he criticizes the false teachers: doing so parallels the rituals of Bacchus. The author of *Jude*, furthermore, points to *Genesis* and *First Enoch* in order to depict such sexual behavior as ungodly, objectionable, and worthy of severe punishment. The offending angel most associated with this sacrilegious sexual behavior takes the form of a goat. Bacchus also takes the form of the goat. Thus, a whole cluster of parallels exists between (1) the discussions in *Jude* and (2) the nature and practice of the cult of Bacchus. These parallels, presented in Table 5.1, are so many that they do not appear to be the result of mere coincidence.

Table 5.1: A Connection With Bacchus: The Evidence

	Issue	**Implications**
Motive	The cult of Bacchus faced severe restrictions imposed by the Roman government. Ending restrictions would have been welcomed by and helpful to the cult.	Initially, Christianity was viewed as a part of Judaism and granted freedom of worship. By merging with Christianity, the Cult of Bacchus could gain greater freedom of worship.
Similarities	Both Christ and Bacchus are resurrected, connected to wine, are the sons of the dominant God and a mortal woman, their worship involves, cannibalism, etc.	These similarities (coincidental though they were) could have bolstered the beliefs and claims that Christ and Bacchus were the same God.
False Teachings	*Jude* complains about false teachers that encourage licentious sexual behavior in worship and deny the unique divinity of Christ	The cult of Bacchus engaged in ritualistic sexual behavior. Asserting Christ was merely another from of Bacchus denies Christ's unique divinity.
Taboo Mating	*Jude* dwells upon a Biblical story about supernatural beings mating with earthly women to defame his opponents.	The rituals of Bacchus involve and depict supernatural beings and/or their surrogates mating with earthly women.
Goat Image	Azazel, who rebels by mating with earthly women has the form of a goat	Since Bacchus has the form of a goat, the two can be connected in an overt manner.
Discussion	All the evidence points in the same direction to suggest that the *Epistle of Jude* deals with false teachers who attempted to transform Christianity by merging it with the cult of Bacchus. The examples and symbolism used in *Jude* are explicit and the theory that *the Epistle of Jude* specifically rejects the cult of Bacchus must be taken seriously.	

For many years, the *Epistle of Jude* has been dismissed as a general/generic condemnation of false teachers, intertwined with apocalyptic themes. Scholars, however, have indicated that because the evidence is so thin little can be known about the false teachers who are attacked. This paper offers an alternative argument that suggests that the author of *Jude* was concerned with a specific group of false teachers: devotees of Bacchus who wanted to usurp Christianity and transform for its own ends. The evidence for this theory is strong and multi-faceted.

In addition, this interpretation explains why advocates for the early church held the *Epistle of Jude* in such high regard. Early apologists did not praise *Jude* because it provided a pedestrian attack on generic false teachings, but because it marshaled arguments that could be used to counter the threat of a specific Pagan religion that sought to transform Christianity and incorporate Jesus into its pantheon. Early church leaders who confronted a strong Pagan world would have welcomed arguments that provided a means to blunt such threats. Hence, the lavish praise bestowed on this short text.

By the forth century, the *Epistle of Jude* had come to be lumped with 6 other books of the New Testament that were ultimately labeled the "catholic letters." As Connich (1978 351) observes, this term is used to indicate the belief that these documents: "...describe writings composed for the church as a whole in contradistinction to those addressed to particular persons or local congregations.... Whenever "catholic" can be applied appropriately...we are no longer dealing with letters (which have specific audiences) but with epistles (which have general audiences.")

This paper, in contrast, suggests that by the 4th century when the *Epistle of Jude* came to be perceived in this manner, the threat from Bacchus had subsided to such a degree that *Jude* appeared to be a general or catholic treatise even though when written it served a very specific role. The *Epistle of Jude* was not originally a general, generic document, but a response to a particular problem: the threat of a powerful mystery religion that wanted to merge with Christainity.

Today, the issues that the author of the *Epistle of Jude* addressed and the symbolism that was used to do so have become so illusive to the modern reader that the original specific meaning is masked and the epistle appears merely as a general call for morality and faith. This trend in interpretation has resulted in an unfortunate trivialization of an important epistle that affirmed the early church.

References

Anonymous (ND) "Bacchus God of Wine" from internet site
    www.art.nl/journal/ article.aspx?ID=20.
BBC (ND) Dionysus *BBC Religion and Ethic*
    www.bbc.co.uk/print//religion/religions/features/greek_gods/dionysus.shtml

Brown, Raymond E. (1997) An Introduction to the New Testament (New York: Doubleday)

Burckhardt, Jacob (1949) *the Age of Constantine the Great* (Berkeley: University of California Press.)

Harrington, David J. (2003) "Jude and 2 Peter" in *Sacra Pagina* Series Volume 15 (Collegeville, Minnesota: The Liturgical Press) pp161–293.

De Houghton, Charles (1985) "Dionysus" *Man Myth and Magic* Richard Cavendish, editor in chief (New York: Marshall Cavendish.) 583–87.

Leaney, A. R. C. (1967) *the Letters of Peter and Jude* (Cambridge: Cambridge University Press.)

Long, H. S. (2003) Cult of Dionysus (2003) *New Catholic Encyclopedia* (Degtroit: Thompson.)

Lyle, Kenneth (1998) *Ethical Admonition of the Epistle of Jude* (Bern: Peter Land)

Connick, C. Milo (1978) The New Testament: an Introduction to its History Literature, and Thought Second Edition (Encino: Dickenson Publishing Compnay)

Powell, Barry (2001) *Classical Myth*, 3rd edition, Prentice-Hall (New Jersey.)

Rowston, Douglas (1975) "The Most Neglected Book in the *New Testament*", *New Testament Studies* 554–63

"Treading the Winepress: Part 2: The Epiphany of Miraculous Dread" From internet site: www.dhushara.com/book/diochris/ dio2.htm

Discussion of Part 2

The Pragmatics of a Broader Perspective

The three chapters presented above are united by the fact that they center upon the Hellenistic and pagan traditions instead of focusing primarily upon Christianity or upon ways in which the Jews and Gnostics impacted the early church. By doing so, the value of collaborating with and benefiting from classical and/or general religious studies is showcased.

In the 1930s, Biblical scholars tended to turn away from the cross-disciplinary thrust of the "history of religions" school in order to conduct research that was thought to be more relevant to the main concerns of their field. Although this strategy may have led to more appropriate and productive research agendas, it also inhibited investigations in other areas. The three chapters (presented above) point to the fruitfulness of re-embracing a more eclectic style of research and analysis.

Those essays are concerned with a fairly narrow focus (Hellenistic mystery religions and philosophies) and they coincide with my idiosyncratic interests. Nonetheless, these examples demonstrate the value of more forcefully embracing a wider range of perspectives. *Biblical* scholarship is a well established field that touches on many humanistic and liberal arts disciplines. As a result, our field is in a position to contribute, cooperate, and collaborate with diverse partners and do so as an invaluable and equal participant.

Functioning in this manner is in the best interest of *Biblical* scholarship and those with whom we can partner.

Part 3

Giving Back

Prologue to Part 3

Giving Back

A basic premise of this book is that *Biblical* scholars can and should work within the larger intellectual community and give back to it. In Chapters 1 and 2, impressionistic and provocative essays merged *Biblical* scholarship with business strategies. In Chapters 3 though 5, Biblical scholarship was nested with other humanistic disciplines.

Although these chapters are well argued as freestanding chains of thought, they may not adequately demonstrate the full range of how *Biblical* research can contribute to others. This issue needs to be addressed. The last two chapters provide useful perspectives regarding the value of *Biblical* scholarship to both scholars and practitioners even when they do not have an explicit interest in religion.

Because of the slimness of the Christian canon (the *New Testament* is a small library), *Biblical* scholars have developed an array of tools for harvesting and processing as much information as possible from weak clues and thin evidence. Under these conditions, *Biblical* scholars have developed a remarkable intuitive sense and created the tools needed to interpret evidence from a distinct time and place.

A few years ago, I wrote a book on competitive intelligence (Walle 2000) a field of business research that gathers suspect and feeble data and transforms it into useful information. Although some *Biblical* scholars might not feel comfortable within such a private sector context, they would be at home with the actual tasks being performed: culling useable facts from evidence that, at first glance, appears to have little significance. Thus, the tools and insights developed by Biblical scholars may be of value to others who seek to examine weak evidence for latent insights.

In Chapter 6 "Form Criticism and Native Ecology" the ability of form criticism, a major tool of *Biblical* scholarship is expanded to serve new purposes. Although the value of form criticism is debated by *Biblical* scholars, it provides a way to deal with how the process of oral transmission might alter the folkloristic materials that were eventually codified in the *New Testament*.

Form critics stemming, from Herman Gunkel and Rudolph Bultman, recognize that certain "laws" or tendencies of the oral tradition impact how information is remembered and passed from one raconteur to the next. Having expanded techniques from folklore scholarship, form critics gained an ability to analyze what changes had probably taken place in the oral record before the gospels were written down in their final and static form.

This raises an important question: can form criticism serve folklore by contributing the techniques that it has developed? To answer this question, the folklore of a Native American Indian group, (the Winnebago of Wisconsin USA) is examined. Using techniques developed by form and redaction criticism, the sacred oral traditions of this people are examined in a manner that demonstrates how folklorists can benefit from these techniques. Thus, *Biblical* scholarship has much to contribute to other fields and, as a result, it should become more involved in cross-disciplinary collaborations.

Chapters 1 and 2 argue, in a general manner, that *Biblical* scholarship has a role in helping practitioner disciplines. This emphasis upon how *Biblical* scholarship can serve in a practitioner role is further developed in Chapter 7: "The Parables within the Framework of Recovery." This author has earned an academic degree in substance abuse therapy and published a book on the subject (2004) that demonstrates how religious belief can be used as an invaluable tool of recovery. The basic point of that monograph is that religious and spiritual systems embraced by people have a profoundly important role to play in helping counselors and therapists guide clients towards recovery from alcoholism and drug addiction. While that monograph is useful, it deals with Native American religions, not Christianity.

The *New Testament*, a sacred text, can also be employed by practitioners serving alcoholics and substance abusers within the Christian community. In some circumstances, furthermore, the *New Testament*, precisely because of its status as a sacred document, can motivate and inspire. This is dramatized by showing how the parables of Jesus can be reworked in ways that help substance abuse counselors to more effective make key points that are useful to recovery. By doing so, the case is made that *Biblical* scholars can help those in practitioner disciplines to more effectively function within their own professions.

Thus, *Biblical* researchers, besides working within their own disciplines, can help other scholars and practitioners. Although the examples provided are not exhaustive, they demonstrate that *Biblical* scholarship can fruitfully expand beyond its own realm and provide a unique service by doing so.

References

Walle, Alf H. (2000) Qualitative Research in Intelligence and Marketing: The New Strategic Convergence (Westport Connecticut: Quorum Books.)

Walle, Alf H. (2004) The Path of Handsome Lake: A Model of Recovery for Native People (Greenwich, Connecticut: Information Age Publishing.)

Chapter 6

Form Criticism and Native Ecology

INTRODUCTION

Today, much of the traditional heritage of Native, indigenous, and traditional people[1] has been removed from the context in which it was created. In addition, a wide variety of outside cultural, technological, and economic influences increasingly impact these people and their beliefs. As a result, understanding the "true" meaning and significance of a cultural heritage can be illusive. That is especially true of sacred oral traditions.

These cultural heritages are often closely linked to the fact that in the past many Native people participated in a subsistence way of life that was close to nature. Under such circumstances, sacred oral traditions often celebrated Nature. Depending upon the degree of outside intervention (and the character of that contact), the Native heritage may survive either as a vital part of life or in a weakened, fragmented, and vestigial form. In some cases, the heritage of a people may be all but extinct.

In any event, the sacred oral traditions of Native people tend to be very different from the perspectives of modern science and Western[2] thought (that increasingly dominates the world.) The traditional ecological views of Native people, for example, often provide an alternative vision of the world and mankind's role within it. Because this heritage is distinct from and often conflicts with Western, scientific, and "modern" perspectives, it can easily be misinterpreted.

---

[1] For simplicity, the "Native people" will be used hereafter.

[2] The term Western, as used in this context, transcends the West and refers to all people who embrace a scientific outlook and other perspectives that stem from the Western heritage, especially that stemming from the Age of the Enlightenment. People who think in this way, of course, come from all over the world over and descend from diverse cultures. Although this terminology is awkward and confusing, it is commonly used and will be continued here for that reason.

In this paper, form criticism, a specific tool of exegesis, is adapted for use when analyzing Native oral traditions. This is followed by a test case in which the method is applied to a sample of traditional Native texts.

A discussion of the liberal theologians of the 19th century who gave a one-sided and distorted interpretation of sacred Christian texts provides a useful orientation. The discussion continues by demonstrating that sacred oral traditions of Native people are likely to be misinterpreted in a manner that parallels the thought of these liberals. Ways in which form criticism can help prevent these misconceptions are discussed. After this toolkit has been "roughed out", a sample application of the method is provided.

Distortions of Christian Liberalism

The late 19th century was an era in which people tended to believe in "progress" and the perfectibility of people and their institutions. The optimism associated with social Darwinism, furthermore, pointed to a better life for all people and to a more moral and rational future for mankind. These ideas seemingly implied that people possess the ability to take control of their own destiny and to work in ways that achieve God's goals. Such sentiments created an environment where theologians interpreted the religious heritage of the Christian community in ways that somewhat de-emphasized divine intervention while simultaneously encouraging the belief that people can create a 'heaven on earth.'

This was also an era when many Biblical scholars sought to discover the "historic Jesus" by examining the sacred writings and traditions of Christianity. One aspect of this heritage is a recurring apocalyptic theme that emphasizes that God has total control and that salvation is a gift from the divine, not the fruit of human effort. Such views, however, were in direct conflict with the ideas of progress and the belief in the perfectibility of mankind that dominated 19th century liberal thought.

As a result, many liberals ignored or explained away the apocalyptic message of the scriptures. As an alternative, these thinkers depicted the apocalyptic content of the Bible merely as a metaphor or mode of expression, viewing it as an artifact of ancient times that had little theological importance. The real message of the *Bible*, they asserted, stressed themes such as the belief that God is the father of all mankind, that people need to love one another, that every human being/soul has a profound worth, etc.

Interpreting Christianity and its sacred texts in this manner, the apocalyptic theme was underplayed and largely dismissed. Adolph von Harnack (1901) gives a classic presentation of this orientation. According to his view, Jesus was a wonderful teacher whose message mirrored the liberal beliefs of the age. Other theologians such as James Orr (1902) (see McGrath (1996) and A. B. Bruce (1881), in tandem with such perspectives, asserted that when people acted according to God's will, his reign would begin. A basic premise of this orientation is that the fruit of such initiatives would be a paradise on earth, created by and established through human effort.

While many 19th century scholars sought to discover the historic Jesus, their vision tended to be a mirror of their own 19th century liberal views. Although the thinkers who embraced this point of view conceded that God may be needed to provide leadership and moral guidance, they assumed that much of the work of creating a paradise on earth falls upon the people themselves.

While this was a powerful and influential chain of thought that was reinforced by the spirit of the age, it was not to remain unchallenged. Most pointedly, Albert Schweitzer dismissed these liberal interpretations by demonstrating that Jesus clearly embraced strong apocalyptic orientations and believed that mankind could not change the world nor control its destiny. In point of fact, the Bible that has come down to us clearly states that Jesus emphasized that salvation and paradise would not come be the result of human effort, but was the gift of divine intervention.

Repudiating the quest to discover the historic Jesus on the grounds that scholars were reading their own views into their vision of the Lord, Albert Schweitzer (in an oft-quoted statement) concluded that "Jesus as a concrete historic personality remains a stranger to our time." (Schweitzer (1911 399.)

In doing so, Schweitzer observed that Jesus is not viewed on his own terms, but is interpreted from the vantage point of the modern era. He complained that the musings of the theologians of his day ignored the Biblical record that emphasizes that (1) Jesus had a strong apocalyptic orientation and (2) that Jesus envisioned an almost immediate end of the world due to the intervention of God (Schweitzer 1911.) Biblical scholars continue to view Schweitzer's work as seminal even if some temper his findings.

Schwietzer emphasized that while texts are created in their own time and place, they are often interpreted outside of that context. He stressed that because 19th century liberal scholars embraced a particular world view, they had trouble objectively viewing and interpreting events that took place in the era when the *New Testament* was written.

A Similar Problem with Native Studies

The way that Jesus was distorted by 19th century liberals demonstrates that people tend to interpret sacred knowledge with reference to their own needs, situations, worldviews, and agendas. As we have seen, this led 19th century theologians to paint a picture of Jesus that reinforced the belief that mankind was evolving to a higher plane of existence and that people could reach perfection largely through their own efforts. These views, although noble and inspirational, constitute a serious misreading of the sacred texts of Christianity, a situation that demonstrates how distortions can creep into the interpretation of sacred text (oral or written) if they are viewed from outside of a "proper" context.

The sacred oral traditions of Native people can be misinterpreted in a similar way.

A classic example of this potential is the acclaimed *Wisdom of the Elders* by David Suzuki and Peter Knudtson (1992.) One reason for choosing this book is the fact that the authors (actually compilers and editors) have great respect for Native people and their intellectual heritage. Although Suzuki and Knundtson are friendly to Native people and their heritage, they interpret the sacred thought of these people in a manner that serves the needs of the modern world, not those who created the texts.

Indeed, the authors use Native oral traditions to advance their own agenda: promoting the ecology movement. Suzuki and Knundtson juxtapose the thoughts of modern ecologists from the modern industrialized world with a carefully selected sample of Native thought. Distortions occur when the sacred oral traditions of Native people are used to advance a modern ecological agenda. As a result, *Wisdom of the Elders* fails to present the traditions of Native people on their own terms. However noble their mission might be, Suzuki and Knundtson manipulate the words of Native people in order to achieve their own goals and promote their own worldview.

Throughout the book, Suzuki and Knundston use the comments of various Native people (interlaced with quotations of partisan Western scientists) in order to discuss the looming ecological crisis. The perspectives of various Native people are showcased as examples of a grassroots understanding of ecological truths that have seemingly been forgotten by contemporary Western and industrialized decision-makers. In one example from Chapter 2, a discussion of the Desana of Columbia is preceded by a quotation by Lynn Margulis, a biologist who notes that evolution is characterized by both cooperation and competition. This observation is followed by a thumbnail sketch of Desana life and a brief overview of some mythological beliefs that underscores the idea that all things are interconnected. Suzuki and Knudtson go on to assert that this mythology closely resembles what we now call "biological equilibrium." The authors make this claim after removing Native knowledge from its indigenous context and reworking it to serve the needs of the modern, industrialized world. Although space does not permit a detailed discussion of their work and the many other similar examples to be found there, Suzuki and Knudtson repeatedly rip the sacred oral traditions of Native people from their context, juxtapose them with pithy quotes from ecologically minded Western scientists, and equate the two streams of thought. Although their book has laudable sentiments, it distorts the sacred oral traditions of Native people in ways that serve the eidtor's agendas (in a manner that parallels how 19th century liberal theologians distorted Jesus.)

In our discussion of Albert Schweitzer, we saw how 19th century liberals misread the sacred texts of Christianity in ways that reinforced their worldview by suggesting that Jesus believed mankind could create a heaven on earth. Suzuki and Knundtson move in an opposite direction by misinterpreting Native traditions in order to underscore their belief that modern people are creating a hell on earth. The same mistake is made in both cases: sacred traditions are misinterpreted by partisan people who consciously seek to advance a particular point of view. Such tactics cannot be defended, no matter how noble the cause being served in the process.

Form Criticism: A Thumbnail Sketch

In the 20th century, Christian theologians became increasingly interested in understanding how their sacred texts came into existence. They recognized that although the *Bible* is based in part upon actual events, it was also written at a particular time and within a specific context. As a result, scholars sought to understand what the people who wrote (and first heard) these documents thought and felt. How did the books of the *New Testament* (especially the synoptic gospels) fit into and resonate from the environment in which they were created?

The new method of analysis that arose recognized that the sacred texts of Christianity are complex documents that are based, in part, upon an oral tradition. Until crystallized and petrified by pen and paper, these oral traditions would have been available for conscious and/or unconscious editing by those who preserved the memories of Jesus and the early Church. Scholars such as Rudolph Bultman became increasingly interested in this process and its implications. For present purposes, it is worthwhile to note that both the synoptic gospels and many Native traditions derive from an oral tradition. As a result, tools of analysis that were created by *Biblical* scholars to deal with the impact of oral transmission upon Christian sacred texts can be adapted for examining the Native heritage.

The "form criticism" that developed to serve in this capacity has a long history. Those seeking an overview of the method and its history are referred to John Hayes *Biblical Form Criticism and its Content* (1974.) Gene Tucker (1971) provides a useful overview of the manner in which form criticism takes place. In specific, he enumerates four steps or processes that commonly occur including:

1. The structure or pattern of the particular communication is analyzed.

2. Based on this analysis, it is evaluated as part of a specific genre.

3. The historic and social setting of the document is discussed.

4. The purpose or intent of the communication is analyzed.

One of the initial benefits of form criticism (when it arose in the early 20th century) is that it provided a way to expand beyond the conventional methods of literary criticism that focus upon the personality, skill, and creativity of a particular author. Many of the sacred documents in the Bible, in contrast, do not have an identifiable "author" and/or these documents evolved over a significant period of time. Apparently, bits and shards of the oral tradition were routinely used as raw material and incorporated into the written texts. As a result, these documents were profoundly influenced by a variety of pre-existing oral traditions and they are not merely the product of one creative mind or a unique author.

One of the pioneers of form criticism is Hermann Gunkel who emphasizes, "...we must...have the whole situation before us and ask ourselves Who is Speaking? Who are the listeners? [what venue is used when the communication is made?]... What effect is aimed at?" (1928 62.)

Rudolph Bultman, perhaps the most respected of all form critics, was very interested in the literary heritage of preliterate societies. As McCartney and Clayton (2002) have observed, Bultman was aware that: "...in primitive societies, the mythology and legends of that society are a dynamic store of lore, which grows and adapts itself to ever changing situations. The oral "literature" of such groups is thus constantly relevant." (McCartney and Clayton 2002 104.)

McCartnehy and Clayton continue by observing that:

Bultman...began to look at the Gospels not for historical materials about Jesus, but for indications of how... [people] used the traditions about Jesus.

> To do this meant identifying within the Gospels the pieces of the oral
> tradition that were elaborated, and asking how such elaborations met the
> needs of the [people] (104-5.)

The legacy of form criticism offers two additional perspectives that are useful within the context of Native studies. They include what is commonly known as the "criterion of dissimilarity" and "redaction criticism." Each is briefly discussed.

The criterion of dissimilarity observes that those who created the *New Testament* had no motive to preserve details of Jesus that did not reinforce the beliefs and principles of the church. Just the opposite, they might have sought to edit out this material or soften its impact. Authors, in contrast, would have a motive to invent, repeat, or emphasize content that reinforced the dogma of the church. Although scholars cannot dismiss Jesus' actions and beliefs simply because they jive with the dogma that was emerging, the oral transmitters had a vested interest in presenting such material. As a result, such content must be viewed with caution.

When statements or actions that are attributed to Jesus do not reflect church dogma, in contrast, the criterion of dissimilarity concludes that they may well be authentic; after all, the authors had no known motive to create such content.

Generalizing this concept, the scholar is directed towards whatever texts do not reflect prevailing traditions and dogma. When deviances from the "conventional wisdom" are observed, the scholar wonders why they were included. One possible reason, of course, is that they might be true and could not be denied. Another might be that they constitute vestigial remains of some sort that have not totally disappeared.

Redaction criticism, another vital tool, emphasizes that authors and compilers of the gospels were strategically thinking and goal-oriented individuals. They were working with fluid and evolving oral traditions and they were writing them down with specific goals in mind. Redaction critics explore how specific people take pieces of a sacred tradition and use within in a specific context to affirm or reinforce a particular point of view. Various stories about Jesus, for example, are retold in different ways within the three synoptic Gospels. Are differences in these retellings merely random occurrences or do they reflect some pattern, motive, strategy, tactic, or cause? Chapter 2 of this book, for example, suggests that the differences in the gospels can be explained with reference to the different target audiences that the authors were addressing. Thus, the authors manipulated their materials in strategic ways to influence specific groups of people. Redaction criticism deals with this process of goal-driven editing.

Redaction critics suggest that authors have certain goals and theological issues clearly in mind. Thus, *Matthew* was created to help convert Jews while *Luke* was written as a public relations document aimed at Roman officials. *Mark*, in contrast, is a relatively simple narrative possessing a minimum of strategic manipulations (Walle 2000.) Redaction critics seek to understand the goals and tactics of an author and interpret a document from that perspective.

The four principles of from criticism discussed above, combined with the criterion of dissimilarity and the method of redaction criticism, provide a rich array of tools that, when properly adjusted, can be applied to studying the sacred oral traditions of Native people.

A Test Case Involving Native Folklore

This chapter seeks to develop and showcase a means of analyzing the cultural the sacred oral traditions of Native peoples within the context of their heritage. It also seeks to deal with the challenges faced by the culture and its people. In order to do so, the techniques suggested by form criticism are generalized and applied to the examination of particular examples of Native mythology.

In specific, variants of a Winnebago[3] myth are examined. Reflecting the analytic style of pioneering form critic Hermann Gunkel, the analysis envisions the "whole situation", takes both the speaker and the listener into account, and seeks to understand the effect of what is communicated (1928 62.)

In specific, these Winnebago myths are analyzed with reference to how that culture related to the environment and to rival groups at different times in its history. The analysis also explores how the oral traditions of the Winnebago evolved over time in tandem with cultural transformations. As was shown above, Rudolph Bultman, a major form critic, was concerned with identifying how sacred oral traditions were transformed in order to meet the needs of the people who heard them. He understood that oral traditions provide a rich variety of materials that can be subtly reworked as conditions change. This chapter examines examples of the Winnebago tradition with these orientations in mind.

---

[3] A Native American people from Wisconsin, United States.

The Evolving Conditions of Winnebago Life

The analysis begins with the observation that over time the impact of the fur trade functioned as a catalyst that transformed the Winnebago from a sedentary society whose livelihood was based on agriculture into a culture made up of small bands who pursued animal pelts that could be sold to White fur traders. This transition from urban farmers to semi-nomadic hunters was a dramatic shift. In large part, this transition was necessary because a sedentary, urban lifestyle and trapping animals are not particularly compatible. In addition, as time went on, the threat of hostile outsiders was reduced and finally eliminated.

Initially, the Winnebago had been a relatively complex culture that was surrounded by rivals who possessed a less complex social structure:

> After entering Wisconsin [in pre-contact times] the Winnebago were completely surrounded by central Algonquian tribes with whom they waged ceaseless war and by whom they were finally forced into the general area of south-east Green Bay. Thus, for three hundred years before the French found them they were in contact with cultures much simpler than their own. In some ways this was fortunate, for it was this fact which enabled them to keep their old culture fairly intact. (Radin 1956 113–4.)

During this pre-contact period, the Winnebago lived in fairly sizable communities: "the villages themselves were relatively large in comparison to historic villages" (Lurie 1960 796.) The economic base during this era was agriculture. "Two Wisconsin informants born in the late 1860s said they had heard of old villages in the Lake Winnebago region where gardens alone had been several arrow shots in breadth" (Lurie 1960 796.)

As might be expected in such a highly organized sedentary community, there was a strong emphasis upon social control and a sophisticated division of labor. Lurie observes:

> A Bear Clan informant explained as late as 1944 that he understood the "police force" function of his clan originated in the very early pre-white period when the Winnebago lived together in villages of several thousand people. They thus required a powerful and highly formulated organization to maintain control over the group (1960 796.)

After White contact, however, Winnebago society, social structure and settlement patterns radically changed and much of its heritage was rendered obsolete. In the course of a few decades, the economic base was transformed from agriculture to one of trapping and trading furs to the French.

The Winnebago's complex social organization, furthermore, was not well suited to this new economic situation and:

> it is possible that the central Algonkain tribes were better able to accommodate themselves to the requirements of the fur trade than were the Winnebago when the Ottawa [who came to trade] first appeared with goods of French origin. The Algonkians were already organized in terms of local bands and relied largely on hunting before the fur trade was introduced (Lurie 1960 796.)

As trading for French goods became increasingly important, the Winnebago evolved to take advantage of this opportunity. The Winnebago's historic reliance upon agriculture and village life would have limited the people's knowledge the environment and the habits of fur bearing animals. As the people became increasingly dependent upon living off the bounty of the land, however, the culture was adjusted and people relocated from centralized towns to a more dispersed settlement pattern. "A general diminution of game through the 18th century contributed to a further scattering to local groups" (Lurie 1960: 805–6.)

Social scientists routinely observe that White contact often undermines the Native cultures' connection with the local ecological system as the people develop a more sedentary and centralized way of life and become dependent upon Western technology. The Winnebago example moves in the opposite situation. Due to White contact, a sedentary people who traditionally lived apart from nature in a manmade environment began to disperse into small bands that lived close to nature in order to trap animals. This new vocation demanded a subtle understanding of the environment. Thus, Winnebago culture was transformed towards, not away from, an understanding of the natural environment and the wild animals that lived there.

Among other trade goods, the Winnebago had access to guns and, as a result, they gained the upper hand in their conflict against the Algonkian. Due to this advantage, the Winnebago displaced their rivals and, thereby, eliminated the threat of attacks by outside forces. This freedom from fear made it even more possible to live in remote circumstances close to nature.

With the Algonkian threat eliminated, the Winnebago continued to evolve away from highly organized towns towards small settlements that existed within the natural environment. In pre-contact times there was a:

> ...single chief over large numbers of people...these generalizes views of chiefianship are steill expressed by reliable informants. However, during the treaty period in the early 19th century, the Winnebago clearly practices a

system of leadership based on the local group. Each band chief exercised his sway over his own community (Lurie 1960 796-7.)

In essence, the coming of White trade goods and the need to reorganize the economy around earning these goods rendered the traditional social organization of the Winnebago obsolete. In addition to changing settlement patterns, the new economic realities demanded that people be increasingly attuned to the smaller, ecological niches where furs could be harvested. Under these conditions, the Winnebago came to live in smaller groups made up of people who depended upon hunting/trapping (a solitary vocation.)

An Early Example of the Winnebago Trickster

As changes triggered by the fur trade took hold, the mythology of the people was adjusted accordingly. New versions of the trickster myth, for example, appeared that were clearly influenced by the new social reality of the post-contact era. In the analysis that follows, two variants of the trickster cycle are compared and discussed in terms of different sets of social conditions that existed when each was created. Concomitant variations between the socio-economic milieu and the world view of the people (as expressed by the texts) are discussed. The changing importance of nature and mankind's relationship to it are explored.

The first example is the trickster cycle as presented by Paul Radin in his *The Trickster* (1956) and elsewhere (1953.) The text basically deals with a "normal individual, the chief of a community" who "takes it upon himself to defy all customs sacred and profane" (1953:336.) As a result of his disregard for the mores of society and social decorum, the trickster figure and those who are dependent upon him suffer. As time goes on, the trickster "attempts to establish a connection with other human beings" (ibid 337), but the socialization process is slow and difficult. Once he is fully integrated with society, however, the trickster is transformed into a respected and honored individual who eventually earns the status of a deity. This story, therefore, emphasizes the benefits that await individuals who act in accordance with the rules that a complex, urban setting demands.

This version of the trickster myth does bear some influence of White contact and contains "a few borrowings from the Whites and from Christianity, beginning with the middle of the 17th century" (Radin 1956 114.) In spite of these obvious influences, however, this version remains the most conservative and traditional text available that was recorded under traditional conditions by a traditional informant who worked directly with Radin and was highly trusted by him. Radin observes, "We can safely assume...that it had the same form 100 years or so ago as it had in 1912 [when gathered]" (Radin 1956 112.) Of all the available texts of the Winnebago trickster cycle, we would expect this variant to exhibit the strongest emphasis upon cooperation and social unity because the Winnebago traditionally lived apart from nature in a highly structured urban setting. As predicted, the text does show these characteristics.

An analysis of this traditional version demonstrates correlations between the plot of the myth and the socio-economic needs of a society that had little connection with nature and little need to understand the local ecology. It, therefore, reflects the traditional, pre-contact culture of the Winnebago. The basic plot emphasizes the benefit of structured and cooperative actions that the traditional Winnebago depended upon for their livelihood. The story also emphasizes the peril of acting in a socially disruptive manner. A knowledge of the environment is not singled out as beneficial.

The plot of this traditional version is presented in Table 6.1:

Table 6.1: The Winnebago Trickster Cycle: A Traditional Example

Component	Description	Analysis
Error in Strategy	Person defies all customs, sacred and profane (Radin 1953 336)	Story derives from era when people lived in towns and where the ability to function individual needed to function within nature was not highly prized
Negative Results	He finds himself wandering aimlessly from place to place (Radin 1953 337)	Defying the established customs of a highly structured community results in the trickster being forced to wander.
Wise Strategy	Embarks on process of regaining contact with people (Radin 1953 337–8)	The process of reuniting with society is long and difficult.
Positive Results	Reunites with society. Becomes a god who helps mankind (1953 338)	The rewards of acting in ways that reinforce the highly structured society are depicted.
Discussion	The traditional trickster cycle focuses upon the needs of a highly organized society that lived within a mankade environment. The personality and skills of those who were individualistic and live close to nature are not highly valued.	

The traditional version of the trickster myth deals with a specific personality type (outsider/individualist) and the results of his asocial behavior. Not until the trickster's personality and behavior conform to the needs of a complex and highly organized society does he meet with success and gain the respect of others. The traditional myth, therefore, explicitly discusses behavior strategies that are appropriate and inappropriate within the pre-contact cultural context that was sedentary, urban, and required minimal interaction with nature. Social and cooperative actions are lauded while individualistic and asocial behaviors (that might have value if living close to nature) are depicted as counterproductive.

A Later Variant

The full implications of this traditional plotline are not fully apparent, however, until it is compared to a later post-contact version that reflects the impact of the fur trading era.

This later and less traditional version is the tale "Turtle Tries to Get Credit" that Radin calls a modern production (1926: 26.) According to Radin, the influence of the older trickster cycle is obvious and the hero "is trickster and all the characteristics that are associated with him in the trickster cycle are found here. He is untrustful, boastful, and a gambler" (1926 26.)

Radin clearly understood that this tale was an example of literary evolution in a changing cultural and environmental milieu. He observes, "The story is interesting because it makes clear the fact that the redactor-authors use the figures of the older mythology in the modern tales, and that new stories are continually constructed" (Radin 1926 26.) A close examination of "Turtle Tries to Get Credit" reveals the older mythic form has been rephrased to deal with a new social and economic context. The new skills (trapping and trading) and the new social attitudes (individualism and social disunity) are emphasized and celebrated.

The basic plot of this modern trickster text involves an individualistic Winnebago who cannot get credit from the fur traders who refuse to provide aid because of the trickster's asocial behavior. One poor, but kindly fur trader saves Turtle and his family from cold and hunger. As the story progresses, Turtle demonstrates that he has superior skills and that his knowledge of nature and his ability to work in isolation are ideally suited to the economic realities that the people face. As a result, the kindly fur trader becomes rich and Turtle gains prosperity, honor, and emerges as a de facto White. This version actually has two intertwining plots: one emphasizes that the Winnebago need to live closer to nature while the other provides a model regarding how fur traders should deal with the Winnebago. The tale can be expressed in the Table 6.2:

Table 6.2: Turtle Tries to Get Credit

Component	Winnebago Subplot	Fur Trader Subplot
Error in Strategy	The Winnebago use collective methods and move in mass to the best hunting grounds. This is a poor strategy because large numbers of people scare animals away	The fur traders refuse to deal with the loner/outsider. "Turtle went to the traders, but they all refused" (1926 46
Negative Results	Negative situations develop when nature is not understood. "He tried to use the sticks that had been used before, but they were frozen and brittle and the one men had not permitted them to dry" (1926 51.)	Fur traders who wouldn't help the individualist who understands nature do not profit from his success. Ater winning a rich catch, he affirms "I won't sell any of them [the furs\] to you."(1926 52.)
Wise Strategy	Turtle acts in a way that disregards conventional tactics and he exhibits an individualism that is close to nature (Radin 1926 48.)	One fur trader gives aid and support to the individualistic outsider who is close to nature. "I am going to give you a little credit" (1926 47.)
Positive Results	Turtle becomes rich, honored, and a de-facto White. "He has brought back many furs. They decorated him. Turtle remained in possession of the store." (1926 52)	Fur trader who gave credit to the individualist who is close to nature becomes rich (Radin 1926 52.)
Discussion	The whole emphasis of this variant of the Trickster myth is that those who are adapted to live in a manmade environment are not up to the task of trapping. Those who can embrace nature, in contrast are able to meet with success and win respect. Thus, the story celebrates those who have an understanding of the ecology of the region	

This later text is clearly of heuristic value in demonstrating the pragmatics of a new economic reality in which "culturally disordered they [the Winnebago] reformed their socio-economic patterns around the pursuit of peltry animals" (Lurie 1960 804-5.) In addition, and of especial importance, is the fact that the new economic realities brought by the fur trade caused the Winnebago to become concerned with the broad ecological system, not merely with made a manmade environment that facilitated agriculture involving domesticated plants.

A Comparison

In both stories, the major character remains unchanged. The trickster figure is always a loner, a challenger, and a breaker of traditions. The fate of the trickster, however, is radically different in the two stories and the transformation of the plot formula reflects changing socio-economic conditions and the need for the Winnebago people to be aware of the ecology of the region in order to earn their livelihood. When people lived an urban life and were dependent upon agriculture, the trickster's asocial behavior was portrayed as counter productive. When the economy became more dependent upon the ecology of the region, however, the individual's asocial/loner personality, coupled with a sophisticated knowledge of nature, were celebrated.

In both stories, the trickster is presented as a role model who showcases successful ways of living. As conditions changed, however, so did the message.

A Form Criticism Analysis

As indicated above, form criticism focuses upon viewing texts from within the context in which they originally existed. By doing so, it may be possible to avoid misinterpretation due to inappropriate analyses that are forced upon the text. Originally a branch of Biblical scholarship, form criticism developed a four-fold approach that will be applied to the Winnebago trickster cycle in a brief test case of how the method can be used in research involving folklore and Native studies. The four fold approach to analysis is presented below.

The structure or pattern is analyzed.

The analysis of two variants of the trickster cycle demonstrates a similarity and the existence of recurring patterns. The protagonist of both stories exhibits an identical personality type: strong willed, individualistic, and asocial. The trickster defies convention and he does things in his own way. In both stories, the hero shows disrespect for authority and tradition.

The structure of both stories revolves around the impact of such patterns of behavior as the hero finds himself in conflict with the greater society. Radin realizes that the two stories have a similar pattern or structure and he observed that the "figures of the older mythology [are used] in the modern tales" (Radin 1926 26.) This recurring pattern or plotline can be depicted, most generally, in Table 6.3:

Table 6.3: The General Structure of the Trickster Story

Component	Description	Analysis
Error in Strategy	The Trickster cycle showcases errors in strategy that prove to be detrimental.	In a highly structured social environment, going against the collective will is negatively depicted. In a world that is close to nature and demands individual action, collective tactics are depicted as counterproductive
Negative Results	The error in strategy leads to negative results.	When collective action was highly prized, acting individually led to crisis. When the economy depended on upon individualistic actions and knowledge of the local ecology, acting collectively and being ignorant of nature led to crisis.
Wise Strategy	A pattern of response that reflects the needs of the people is embraced.	People acted in ways that reflect the needs of the people and the economy.
Positive Results	The results of this strategy benefits both society and the specific individuals who exhibit this strategy.	People who act in a way that is appropriate, given the conditions, are successful and honored.
Discussion	In both cases, the Trickster cycle dramatizes the needs of the people and society. Heroes evolve towards achieving the goals of society in an appropriate and effective manner and in a way that mesh with the economic realities of the era	

Both variants exhibit patterns of behavior that were effective and appropriate in a particular time and place. Thus, the stories possess the didactic value of showcasing constructive strategies of behavior at two different times in Winnebago history.

Evaluated as part of a specific genre.

Both stories are examples of a mythic tale that deals with a particular character or heroic type: the trickster. Trickster tales were commonplace and constitute a specific genre of oral literature among the Winnebago and many other Native American peoples. The first story is an obvious example of the classic trickster story. Radin affirms that the second story is a modern variant based on the legacy of the trickster cycle (1926 26.)

The trickster cycle deals with a certain type of people: individuals who are asocial and loners. Trickster stories deal with their adventures and misadventures as they struggle in the world. The original audiences would have recognized both stories as being a part of this genre.

Situations where a genre evolves over time can be usefully examined using form criticism. The method, as discussed above, acknowledges that traditional societies possess oral traditions that can be adjusted as circumstances change. Being relatively fluid because they do not exist in a "fixed" written form, these oral traditions can be constantly manipulated and transformed to maintain their relevance in a changing world (McCartney and Clayton 2002 104.)

The historic and social setting is discussed.

The historic or social settings of the two variants of the trickster genre are very different. The earlier story is a product of a complex, urban society in which the economy was based upon a manmade environment. The people did not live close to nature and, apparently, they saw little benefit in doing so. People who lived in this era would have viewed the asocial loner as socially disruptive, counterproductive, and as a drain upon society.

The second story took place in a society in which the settlement patterns were less urban and were increasingly typified by small bands. This emerging social structure was better able to exploit the local environment. The economy, furthermore, was based upon nature, not a manmade environment. In such a situation, the individualist innovator who lived close to nature would have been depicted as a role model to emulate.

The purpose or intent is analyzed

Although at a superficial and ad hoc level, stories are told for entertainment, recurring plotlines typically have some kind of educational value. In line with this didactic role, the analysis of the evolving Winnebago trickster myth has shown that during the era when they were performed both variants provided useful insights regarding how to live successfully in Winnebago society.

The first story is a product of a sedentary, urban people who existed within a manmade environment. It emphasizes the importance of being obedient to the rules of society as they existed at a particular point in Winnebago history. In the story, people whose actions do not conform to the realities of Winnebago life suffer. Those who act in concert with the social and economic realities of the era, in contrast, gain respect and prosper.

This traditional story dramatizes the importance of acting in ways that support and reinforce a society that was highly structured and largely divorced from the larger ecological environment. The people, in contrast, concentrated, upon a social structure and an economic base that was linked to a micro, manmade environment.

The second story is the product of a later era in which the settlement pattern of the Winnebago had ceased to be urban and the people were more apt to live in small groups. Instead of living in a manmade environment, people were in closer contact with nature and they needed to understand the ecology of their region in order to earn their livelihood.

This story emphasizes the importance of individual action and it celebrates a knowledge of the ecology of the region. The plot shifts 180 degrees from condemning individualists who are close to the earth to raising them up as heroes and as examples to emulate. In both cases, however, the story presents a role model for members of the original audience.

The technique of the "criterion of dissimilarity", instructs the scholar to pay especial attention to content that does not derive from the pre-existing tradition. In the second trickster story, differences that do not have a significant precedent within traditional Winnebago culture revolve around the positive fate of the individualistic loner who is close to nature. In earlier stories, this type of character had to reform himself around the needs and demands of an urban and highly structured world. In the later story, in contrast, the plot celebrates the skills and abilities of this same kind of person. This is a basic and significance difference that does not derive from the traditional cultural heritage. The "criterion of dissimilarity" points to these differences as particularly important because they demonstrate a shift away from tradition. This shift is mirrored by concomitant changes in the economic life of the people.

This observation leads to the last component of analysis that is based on "redaction criticism": a method that centers upon the conscious or overt intention of the individual creating the particular rendition. Stories often have an educational or instructive value, even if the message is presented in an entertaining and "soft sell" manner. Leaders of the community who told stories would have transformed examples of the traditional mythology in ways that were relevant to the current needs of the people and the community. After the economy and settlement patterns had changed due to the impact of the fur trade, the plotline of the original trickster story would have ceased to provide a useful series of perspectives. As time went on, the stories were adjusted in line with new realities of Winnebago life.

In short, the tools suggested by form criticism can be applied to the study of traditional Native texts that existed within the context of Native society. Such a method is useful in exploring how the Winnebago trickster myth evolved over time. While this analysis has an ad hoc value, it is hoped that the approach suggested here will help others who seek to understand Native traditions on their own terms and explore how these stories evolve in response to changing conditions.

Conclusion

This analysis began by observing that scholars need to be careful not to interpret the sacred oral traditions of Native people from outside of an appropriate context. The work of Suzuki and Knudtson (1992) provides an example of the negative potential of interpreting others from our own perspective. Although these authors are respectful of Native people and although they embrace a laudable point of view regarding protecting the environment, they interpret Native traditions with reference to their own agendas, not the visions of Native people. Doing so needs to be avoided.

Scholars need techniques that facilitate an understanding of Native traditions on their own terms and in ways that prevent distortion. In this paper, methods adapted from form criticism, a technique of *Biblical* scholarship, are used to examine an evolving example of the sacred oral traditions of a particular Native American people. This technique is useful because it takes Native society and its transformation into account when examining an evolving oral tradition.

The methods derived from form criticism are well developed, they have a long intellectual history, and they deal with issues involving cultural change and evolution. As a result, a method derived from this approach has a role in analyzing the sacred oral traditions of Native people. It is hoped that those who examine Native oral traditions will be aware of this methodology from *Biblical* criticism. Although this method and its tools were created to serve in a specific capacity (interpret Christian texts), they possess wider applications. The time has come for these techniques to expand beyond *Biblical* scholarship in order to exert a wider influence upon the larger scholarly community.

References

Boulding, Kenneth (1956) General Systems Theory: The Skeleton of Science *Management Science* V. 2

Bruce, A. B. (1881) *The Chief End of Revelation* (New York: A. D. F Randolph and Company.)

Gunkel, Hermann (1928) *What Remains of the Old Testament* (London: Geroge Allen and Urwin)

Harnack, Adolph von (1901) *What is Christianity?* English translation by Thomas Bailey Saunders (New York: G.P. Putnam.)

Hayes, John (1974) *Biblical Form Criticism and its Content* (San Antinio: Trinity University Press)

Lurie, Nancy O. (1960) "Winnebago Protohistory" in *Culture in History: Essays in Honor of Paul Radin* edited by Stanley Diamond McCartney, Dan and Charles. Clayton (2002) *Let the Reader Understand: A Guide to Interpreting and Applying the Bible*, 2nd edition. (Phillipsburg, New Jersey P & R Press.)

McGrath, Gavin Basil (1999) "James Orr's Endorsement of Theistic Evolution" *Perspectives on Science and Christian Faith* V. 51 # 2 114-21.

Orr, James (1902) *The Christian View of God and the World* (Edinburgh: A. Eliot.)

Schweitzer, Albert (1911) *The Quest for the Historic Jesus*. Translated by W. Montgomery (London: Black.)

Suzuki, David & Peter Knudtson (1992) *Wisdom of the Elders* (New York: Bantam Books)

Tucker, Gene. M (1971) *Form Criticism of the Old Testament* Philadelphia: Fortress Press)

Walle, Alf H. (2000) *Rethinking Marketing* (Westport, Connecticut: Quorum Press.)

Chapter 7

Parables within the Framework of Recovery

Introduction

Substance abuse is a major malady impacting millions of people both directly and indirectly. Great effort is exerted in search of recovery. The stakes are high; and the impact profound.

A classic method that is employed both within self-help activities and during counseling/therapy involves people discussing their challenges, fears, and efforts in meaningful and relevant ways. When doing so, therapists, counselors, clients, and those involved in self-help activities often use stories, metaphors, adages, proverbs, pithy statements, and the like to address key issues of addiction and recovery (see especially O'Reilly 1997 and also Jensen 2000, Warhol and Michie 1996, and Travis 2004.) Doing so often takes the place of more formal techniques counseling, and therapy.

This chapter suggests that the parables of Jesus (classic examples of figurative speech that are well known to many people) have a significant role to play within the dialogue of recovery. This is true because the style that Jesus employed meshes well with techniques of recovery that have long been popular and effective.

Although many of us are familiar with the parables, disagreement exists when people begin to discuss what these literary devices really are. Two ways to evaluate any phenomena are (1) with reference to the categories of analysis that exist within the intellectual community (etic analysis) vs. (2) perspectives that are embraced by the people being examined in research (emic analysis.) This terminology, first coined by Kenneth Pike (1954), has led to heated methodological debates over the years with Pike and his followers advocating the emic approach while others, such as Marvin Harris, championing etic methods (1964, 1968.) Eventually, even Harris, the arch supporter of the etic strategy acknowledged the benefit of both emic and etic techniques when each is used in a responsible and professional manner (1980.)

The etic method analyzes and classifies texts (such as the *Bible* and/or parts of it) accordingly to perspectives suggested by the intellectual community. Those who champion the etic approach, for example, are apt to define terms such as "parables" in formal ways that reflect the traditions of scholarship and the perspectives of researchers. Doing so can be useful. This paper, in contrast, embraces an emic approach and views the communication techniques used in the *Bible* with reference to the feelings and perspectives of those who originally uttered and heard these words. So viewed, the term "parable", as employed in this paper, reflects the wide perspectives embraced by the ancient audience, not merely the musing of contemporary scholars.

Thus, in *Luke* 4: 23 Jesus refers to the short proverb "Physician heal thyself" as a parable (*Jerusalem Bible*.) Indeed, it is commonly agreed that the term "parable" comes from the Greek "paroble" (a Greek word that is broadly applied to refer to some kind of rhetorical comparison.)

Jesus used broad analogies, metaphors, and comparisons (that the ancients lumped together as parables) in order to more effectively communicate with those who would not understand more technical or formal discussions. In *Mark* 4: 11, for example, Jesus says to his disciplines "The secret of the kingdom of God is given to you, but to those who are outside [this group of informed believers] everything comes in parables" (*Jerusalem Bible*.) Thus, Jesus specifically acknowledges that using parables is a valuable technique when providing elementary instruction to the uninitiated.

Jesus also indicated that he spoke using metaphors, analogies, and parabolic speech due to circumstances. In *John* 16:25, for example, Jesus says to his disciples "I have been telling you all this in metaphors, the hour is coming when I shall no longer speak in metaphors; but tell you about the Father in plain words" (*Jerusalem Bible*.) Thus, Jesus spoke in parables/figurative language as required by circumstance and he envisioned this form of communication as a specialized rhetorical technique that was distinctive from "plain speech." As we have seen, Jesus affirmed that parables were particularly effective and appropriate when talking to certain people and/or under specific circumstances.

The author of this article has recently written several books and articles (Walle 2004, 2004a 2007a, 2007b, 2007c that adapt the wisdom of important American Indian religious traditions for use within the context of substance abuse therapy involving Native[4] clients. Doing so is particularly appropriate and relevant to discussions regarding how to use religion within the context of recovery. It demonstrates ways in which a spiritual/religious heritage may serve as a foundation for recovery.

---

[4] The use of Native with a capital "N" indicates the indigenous population. This could include groups such as American Indians, Native Hawaiians, The Maori of New Zealand, and Australian Aborigines.

In this chapter, that method (that was developed within the context of indigenous religious traditions) is employed in ways that serve members of the Christian community. When used among substance abusers who identify with Christianity; the teachings of Jesus can serve as an appropriate and familiar means of addressing issues that arise during the therapeutic process. The strategy of nesting therapy within the context of the Christian heritage can be expected to be particularly effective among those who are comfortable with this religious tradition. Embracing aspects of Christianity within the context of therapy can serve both loyal believers and others who, while not as active within the church, were raised within a Christian context and are familiar with the parables. In some cases where a person is alienated from the Christian religion, of course, making reference to it may be counterproductive; thus, the counselor must use care and judgment when employing religious illusions within the context of therapy.

This analysis is a preliminary attempt to adapt the sacred teachings of the Christian religion in order to help substance abuse counselors to more effectively serve their clients. As indicated above, the method employed is based upon techniques that have previously been used to adjust the teachings of other religious systems so that they can serve as tools of recovery. Having developed this method elsewhere, similar strategies are applied to Christianity: the dominant religion of North America and many other parts of the world.

Systematically Adapting the Parables

The purpose here is to provide the reader with an organized and systematic technique for employing a representative sample of Jesus' parables in a manner that serves the needs of substance abusers seeking recovery. It is hoped that by doing so, substance abuse counselors will be able to more effectively use these Biblical teachings in constructive and therapeutic ways, especially when dealing with clients who come from the Christian tradition.

This work is distinct from scholarship concerning the parables although it is friendly towards and builds upon it. Over the years, a vast amount of material has been written about the parables; limitations of space prevent even the most superficial overview of this wealth of material. Those seeking a greater understanding of this scholarly tradition are urged to consult any number of specialized monographs on the subject. A useful representative sample of materials includes Bailey (1976), Blomberg (1990), Kistemaker (1989), Jones (1984), and Hultren (2000), among others. Jones (1984 1-61) presents a good overview of the scholarly traditions involving the study of the parables; the discussions by Jones' (and others) are recommended to those who seek a review of scholarly trends concerning the parables.

While indebted to formal scholarship, this effort does not exist within that intellectual tradition because it is part of the practitioner literature of pastoral counseling. While seeking to employ the parables in appropriate ways (and, therefore, relying upon scholarship as required), the goal of this paper is to present strategies for using the teachings of Jesus in a circumscribed manner that is dedicated to a particular purpose: helping substance abusers to more effectively recover from their affliction.

The examples analyzed in this paper, furthermore, are illustrative and not exclusive. As a result, I hope that this discussion will encourage individual counselors to develop their own techniques for employing the teachings of Jesus in ways that comfort, instruct, and serve those who struggle with substance abuse and seek recovery.

Applicable in Diverse Settings

The techniques discussed here can be employed in diverse settings. Two basic types of therapy are (1) individual counseling involving a client and counselor in one-on-one interaction and (2) group therapy in which the therapist interacts with an assembly of clients working together as they collectively respond to the challenges of the facilitator and/or to their own self-directed issues. Using the parables of Jesus in order to emphasize key points of recovery can be effective in both contexts. Once disseminated via therapy, adaptations of the parables (that deal with recovery) may become a part of the context of both therapy and self-help within a community. When this happens within a close knit population, the power of the parables as tools of recovery can be expected to grow and merge in synergistic ways with other rhetorical tools of recovery.

Challenges to this Method

Historically, the prevailing model of self-help and therapy aimed as alcoholics has been provided by Alcoholics Anonymous. Indeed, for generations, many people have equated recovery, self-help, and therapy with the "12 Step Program" created by Alcoholics Anonymous. Although Alcoholics Anonymous is not officially a religious organization and takes active steps to deny any religious leaning (by, for example, affirming the program is "spiritual", not "religious"), the founders of the organization came from a Christian background and they were comfortable with their faith. As a result,

Alcoholics Anonymous possesses a covert leaning towards Christianity and it appears to inadvertently embrace key aspects of Christian dogma even though the founders never intended to do so. Thus, the classic literature of Alcoholics Anonymous overtly encourages members (and potential members) to believe in any God they choose, and phraseology such as "God as we understood him" is employed in order to avoid any appearance that the organization is sectarian. Nonetheless, the literature of Alcoholics Anonymous describes God as personal, caring, rational, male, etc. in ways that bring the God of the Jewish, Christian, and Islamic believers to mind. Under these circumstances, religious dogma and specific programs of recovery can easily become intertwined. Those who agree with AA's generic depiction of God will probably not object to these parallels. Others, however, may balk.

In recent years, various programs of treatment have been developed in order to create alternative methods of recovery that do not (overtly or covertly) embrace a religious orientation. The founders of such programs often state they are doing so in order to provide alternatives to the religious ethos of Alcoholics Anonymous and its 12 Step Program. Representative methods that overtly seek to provide recovery without a reliance upon religion include the work of Christopher (1992, 1997), Hovarth (1997), and Trimpey (1985), etc. Such methods have been developed because their advocates believe that faith-based strategies of recovery are not effective (and may even prove to be counterproductive) when practiced by at least some people.

These secularizing efforts are designed to insure that people have access to therapy that is appropriate for them. Making these tools available is applauded. While some people may be disserved by a religious content within therapy, however, those who possess a strong religious focus may benefit from employing aspects of their faith as tools of recovery. When this is the case, religion and aspects of it (such as the parables of Jesus) may serve as powerful tools of therapy, self-help, and recovery. Appropriately employed, these tools have a legitimate role in such circumstances.

Those who are critical of religion wish to empower secular people who seek recovery; they do so by offering methods of therapy that are stripped of any religious veneer. I agree with these goals and the logic underlying them. Having said this, it is equally important to recognize that many people relate to the world with reference to their Christian heritage. Their religion provides these people with comfort, strength, and guidance. Just as providing secular people with tools of recovery that suit their needs is appropriate, adapting the Christian tradition in relevant ways to better serve believers is entirely proper, professional, and responsible (as long as these techniques are applied to a relevant manner.)

To help achieve such a goal, ten of Jesus' parables are discussed as tools of recovery. More broadly, the paper suggests that a wide variety of Biblical materials can be presented in ways that facilitate treatment, self-help, and recovery.

Representative Parables to be Used

The parables of Jesus are powerful tools of instruction. Here, I have selected a convenience sample of his teachings to show how inventive therapists can present principles of recovery with reference to the client's religious heritage.

The ten parables to be considered include "the Prodigal son", "the Barren Fig Tree", "the Laborers in the Vineyard", "the Mustard Seed", "the Wise and Foolish Builders", "the Pharisee and the Tax Collector", "the Seed Growing Secretly", "the Parable of the Tower", "the Parable of the Sower, and "the Great Pearl" Each is discussed below.

Parable # 1: "The Prodigal Son": *Luke* 15: 11–32

The parable of the prodigal son will probably have special meaning to many substance abusers because it concerns a wastrel who squanders his legacy in a drunken and sinful orgy while simultaneously shaming his family. Destitute, the man returns home hoping to merely be treated as a servant, so he will not starve to death. To his surprise, the prodigal son is completely forgiven by his father and his return is celebrated with a lavish feast. The brother of the prodigal son, however, finds it impossible to forgive and forget. Thus, the parable reminds those seeking recovery that while they may be able to regain the love of some that they have hurt, others will be more resistant to reconciliation.

As indicated above, this parable can be used to affirm that some people are able to forgive while others are not. Those in recovery need to reach out and make amends, on the one hand, while recognizing that some people may rebuff them, on the other. The counselor can adjust the use of the parable as required. Under certain circumstances, the ability for some people to forgive may be emphasized. On other occasions, the client may be warned that not all people will be able to overlook the past. Reminding clients of this possibility is important so they can cushion disappointments. A well-rounded presentation will emphasize that some people easily and quickly forgive, while others do not. These are vital issues that those seeking recovery often need to address.

Those who are being prepared to make peace with those they have hurt in the past can benefit from this parable. On many occasions, furthermore, the counselor may sense that the issues of forgiveness or lack of forgiveness need to be considered. Under these circumstances, a discussion of the parable may prove to be useful. The essence of the parable and its application are presented in Table 7.1:

Table 7.1: "The Prodigal Son": Forgiveness and Non-Forgiveness

Parable	Application	Uses
Prodigal Son	Can be used in situations where the client needs to be reminded that many people are capable of forgiveness. The parable also affirms that some people may not be able to forgive. This is a much loved parable and very relevant to substance abuse since the protagonist was apparently a substance abuser who lived a wild and sinful life. Some clients in recovery may identify with him.	1 Underscore the possibility of forgiveness, 2 Remind client that not all will forgive 3 Emphasize that those in recovery may face circumstances where both forgiveness and a continued resistance to forgive may exist within the same family/group. 4 Stimulate discussions regarding how to deal with tensions within the family/group.
Discussion	The parable of the "Prodigal Son" deals with both forgiveness and the fact that some people may not forgive and/or take a longer time in order to extend forgiveness. Almost all people with a Christian background are familiar with this parable and, therefore, it can be used almost universally.	

The parable of the Prodigal Son is well known and much loved. It provides a way for the counselor to deal with the issues of forgiveness and non-forgiveness. Used in therapy, it can prepare clients both for the support they may receive from others as well as with the disappointment that may occur when attempts at reconciliation fail.

Parable # 2: "The Barren Fig Tree" *Luke* 13: 1–9

The parable of the "Barren Fig Tree" concerns a fig tree that has never borne fruit. The owner of the orchard wants to cut it down. The foreman, however, asks for more time saying he will better prepare the roots and fertilize the soil to give the tree another chance for success. The past poor performance of the tree is overlooked and the decision is made to judge it with reference to future performance, not with an eye towards previous failures.

This parable affirms that some people are willing to give a second chance to those who have disappointed them in the past. Many substance abusers are depressed and embarrassed because of their past failures. On some occasions, these people have committed "sins of omission" and failed to do what they should have. On other occasions, people have performed acts that are clearly unacceptable. Under the influence of drugs and alcohol, for example, substance abusers often squander their paychecks; steal to feed their habit; act in abusive manners; indulge in illicit relationships; etc.

Some people will overlook past failures, others will not. This reality needs to be addressed. The fact that people who have been unproductive may gain the ability to contribute also needs to be emphasized. This parable of the "Barren Fig Tree" can be used within these contexts.

An overview of the "Barren Fig Tree" can be presented in Table 7.2:

Table 7.2: "The Barren Fig Tree": Patience vs. Impatience

Parable	Application	Uses
Barren Fig Tree	The parable can be used to deal with the fact that those seeking recovery often have a long history of underachievement and irresponsible behavior. They need to be reminded that while some may be willing to give them another chance, others hesitate to do so.	1 Remind the client that some people will be willing to give those who sincerely seek recovery a second chance. 2 Remind the client that others will not easily forgive and forget. 3 Encourage the client to believe in him/herself.
Discussion	The parable of the "Barren Fig Tree" is forward looking and it encourages people to think of the future, not the past. Many people seeking recovery have a history of underachievement and irresponsible/hurtful behavior. They need to avoid dwelling upon their past track record and envision a more productive future. People seeking recovery also need to remember that while some may be willing to offer a second chance, others are more resistant. Those seeking recovery also need to focus upon their ability to change and not allow past failures to emerge as a self-fulfilling prophesy. The parable can be used to address such issues.	

Thus, the parable of the Barren Fig Tree" can be used to address the fact that while some may give others a second chance, others resist doing so. Nonetheless, progress is possible; those seeking recovery need to be forward looking and not dwell upon past failures.

Parable # 3: "Laborers in the Vineyard": *Matthew* 20: 1–16

"The Laborers in the Vineyard" suggests that people should be judged by who they are, not by how long they have been that way. In the parable, different bands of laborers are hired at various times of the day; thus some have worked longer than others. At the end of the day, however, they are all paid the same amount This appears to be unfair to those who have worked long and hard, but if viewed by the fact that all ended up as good and productive contributors, their equal treatment is fair and equitable. Many alcoholics and substance abusers have lived unproductive and even sinful lives. Can they ever stand shoulder to shoulder to other people and look them straight in the eye? The answer is yes! Just as the workers who came to the vineyard in the afternoon were ultimately treated on a par with those who started early in the morning, those who gain sobriety deserve respect and equal treatment as long as they remain "clean and sober" and live in a productive manner. This parable can be used to encourage clients to focus on the future and to recognize that they potentially have an equal place within it. The parable can also be used to reason with those who have been hurt in the past by substance abusers in order to affirm that these people should be treated on a par with others as long as they deserve it. Some people may be resentful when former substance abusers are treated on a par with them. Coming to grips with this possibility is important.

Table 7.3: Laborers in the Field

Parable	Application	Uses
Laborers in field	The parable provides a way to emphasize that those in recovery deserve to be evaluated with reference to who they are, not how long they have been that way. The parable also emphasizes that some people, especially those with a long track record of responsibility may be resentful of those who come to sobriety late but are treated on a par with them.	1 Affirm that recovering people should be judged by who they are , not by what they were. 2 Acknowledge that some people may resent this situation and not want to give parity to someone who has been sober for a relatively short time. 3 Provide a context where people can talk about their resentments in a way that can lead to a positive reconciliation.
Discussion	People should be judged by who they are, not by how long they have been that way. Those seeking recovery, however, need to be reminded that others may be resentful when the newly sober are treated as full fledged equals.	

The "Laborers in the Field" emphasizes that coming late to sobriety does mean that a person should be treated as a second class citizen. While this is true, the parable also emphasizes that others may be resentful when latecomers are treated on a par with them. In spite of such hard feelings, however, people in recovery need to be judged by who they are, not with reference to what they were in the past.

Parable # 4: "The Mustard Seed": *Matthew* 13:31–2

Many people who are first attempting to recover from substance abuse may not believe that they will be able to restructure their lives in a positive, constructive, and productive manner. Those who have suffered a relapse may be even more discouraged. This lack of belief in the possibility of success can be a major obstacle to recovery because people are unlikely to devote strong efforts to a task that they do not believe can be accomplished.

The parable of the "Mustard Seed" can be useful within such contexts. It affirms that sober/right living (in the *Bible*, behaving according to the Kingdom of God) is like a mustard seed (the smallest of and seemingly most insignificant of seeds.) Although small to begin with, the parable tells us that the mustard seed gives rise to a large and productive tree with great strength.

This parable can be used to emphasize that those who have the smallest seed of recovery (or hope for sobriety) in their heart have something that, like the mustard seed, has the ability to grow and mature into something large and powerful. Thus, even those who have failed in the past can be comforted by the fact that even the slimmest motivation can mature into a powerful force that leads to full blown recovery.

Because the small and weak may grow large and powerful, the parable can be a source of inspiration for those who feel discouraged. This message can also be a great comfort when people have inexplicably relapsed and wonder if they will ever enjoy a substantial recovery. People facing this situation are often very depressed and they may lack the confidence they need to practice a program of recovery. The parable can give them hope.

Although relapses are disappointing, they are not the end of the world. Many counselors, furthermore, believe these slips can help client learn from their failures in ways that ultimately provide strength and momentum.

Nonetheless, when people struggle and suffer setbacks they may lose confidence in themselves and in their ability to recover. The Parable of the Mustard Seed provides reassurance when people are discouraged and disappointed in themselves.

Besides helping the client, the "Mustard Seed" can also be used when dealing with people who are involved with the client (such as employers, friends, family, loved ones, etc.) People in these positions often become very discouraged and they may be tempted to "write off" the person as incurable. Under these circumstances, the parable can be used to underscore that where the slightest hope and motivation glimmers the possibility of recovery exists. Like the tiny mustard seed, a small spark of motivation and hope may develop in profound ways that lead to a meaningful recovery.

A tabular presentation of the parable of the Mustard Seed appears in Table 7.4:

Table 7.4: "The Mustard Seed": A little faith can grow in profound ways

Parable	Application	Uses
Mustard Seed	Clients (and those who are involved with them) can gain hope from the parable of the "Mustard Seed", because it can help people to focus upon their progress (small though it may be) and view a first step and as something to build upon.	Motivating clients who are beginning a program of recovery and do not know if they have the strength to succeed. 1 Reassuring clients who have suffered a relapse and are discouraged as a result. 2 Dealing with family members and associates who may be on the verge of giving up on the client.
Discussion	The "Parable of the Mustard Seed" is a very well known. It deals with the fact that hope and motivation have the ability to grow and mature. Thus, even if hope and motivation currently exist only in a small way, they can gain power and strength over time and eventually spearhead a good and productive recovery. This possibility can be very reassuring to clients and their associates.	

The parable of the "Mustard Seed" can be used as a powerful means of interjecting hope into a depressing situation. It is so short and well known that a reference to it can often be interjected into a conversation without breaking the chain of thought, while still making a powerful and compelling statement about the power of hope and motivation.

Parable # 5: "The Wise and Foolish Builders" *Luke* 6:47–9

Many of those seeking recovery have lost a great deal of time, money, respect, etc. and want to restart their lives as quickly as possible. This motivation may tempt some people to take shortcuts that, while leading to apparent progress today, can leave issues unaddressed that will trigger negative results at a later date. The parable of "the Wise and Foolish Builders" the wise builders lay a strong and well constructed foundation for their houses. When trouble comes (a flood) their houses survive. Those who take shortcuts and do not build upon a strong foundation, in contrast, see their homes washed away.)

Those seeking recovery need to restructure their lives upon a strong foundation. These people need time to create a strong foundation upon which to rebuild their lives and establish their recovery. Newcomers are warned that beginning new emotional entanglements before a strong foundation for their lives has been created is courting disaster. People are encouraged to move slowly in order to build a strong foundation. The parable of the "Wise and Foolish Builders" underscores the importance of doing so. It can be used to encourage those in recovery to avoid being impatient and moving too fast. Presented in Table 7.5, the parable emerges as:

Table 7.5: "The Wise and Foolish Builders": Create a strong foundation

Parable	Application	Uses
Wise and foolish builders	People seeking recovery often become impatient when they are asked to work long and hard to accomplish tasks that seem to have no visible or immediate payoff. Doing so, however, may have positive long term results. Counselors often need to encourage people to expend these efforts even though doing so will not immediately change their lives in any overt way.	Valuable when dealing with people who are impatient and want to see immediate progress. Clients may need to be counseled not to be in a hurry Encouraging people to postpone some things until a later date in order to establish a foundation for their sobriety to be built upon.
Discussion	The parable of the "Wise and Foolish Builders" emphasizes that people need to build their recovery upon a strong foundation. If they do not, their progress can be easily swept away. A powerful and resilient foundation, in contrast, can support what is built upon it, including a life in recovery. Although the client may balk at being asked to take an extended time to create this "invisible" foundation, doing so can lead to a lasting and productive recovery.	

Parable # 6: "The Pharisee and the Tax Collector" *Luke* 18:10

Those who seek recovery often face shame. That can impede recovery. The parable of "The Pharisee and the Tax Collector" emphasizes that overly prideful people are often not as noble as those who acknowledge their weaknesses and attempt to overcome them. The parable features a self-serving and egotistical Pharisee (holy man) who brags about his nobleness and thanks God that his is not like the ignoble tax collector. The tax collector, in contrast, is very ashamed of his life, and asks to be forgiven. Jesus tells us that the tax collector is justified in the eyes of God while the Pharisee (who showed all the outward trappings of goodness but lacked them in his heart) is not. Those in recovery may be juxtaposed with others who have not shamed or lowered themselves by falling into a pattern of substance abuse. These people may have "done all the right things" (held jobs, been responsible, been available for their families, not fallen into a pattern of overt sin, etc.) As a result of having not done these things, these people might be prideful and feel superior to those who seek to recovery. The parable, emphasizes that those who acknowledge their shortcomings and ask to be forgiven are more justified and those who merely posture the outward signs of goodness while being arrogant and unable to allow forgiveness to enter their hearts. Table 7.6 abstracts the parable as:

Table 7.6: "The Pharisee and Tax Collector": Humility vs. Pride

Parable	Application	Uses
Pharisee and tax Collector	Those seeking recovery may feel inferior to other people who have not been brought down by drugs and/or alcohol. Associates of the recovering person, furthermore, may view themselves as superior because they have lived "model lives." The parable of the "Pharisee and the Tax Collector" addresses such issues in constructive and powerful ways.	A client may feel inferior due to past behaviors. The parable can be used to emphasize that as long as people recognize their sins, attempt to recover, and ask forgiveness, they can be justified. Sober people often judge others." The parable emphasizes that being overly prideful is more damning that past mistakes.
Discussion	The parable of the "Pharisee and the Tax Collector" can be a very important tool in counseling because many in recovery are judged harshly by others due to their past behavior. Both recovering people and their detractors need to deal with the fact that even those who did bad things in the past can be justified. The sinful nature of being over prideful also needs to be emphasized	

Many people seeking recovery have developed feelings of inferiority due to their behavior while drinking and/or drugging. The associates of these people, furthermore, may feel superior to those in recovery. These are hurtful issues that need to be addressed in forceful ways. The parable of the "Pharisee and the Tax Collector" deals with such issues in a manner that is very relevant to those seeking recovery.

Parable # 7: The seed growing secretly *Mark* 4:26–29

One of the favorite adages of Alcoholics Anonymous is "Don't leave before the miracle happens." The point of this saying is that although a person may be depressed because it appears that no progress is being made, the tools of recovery are often slowly building. If given a chance, they can lead to a strong recovery.

A major stumbling block to recovery, unfortunately, is that progress is often so slow and the results so subtle that many people overlook the subtle strides they are making. Dong so can result in people giving up and embracing a relapse.

The parable of the "Seed Secretly Growing" can be used to reassure clients that suffer from this type self doubt and impatience. The parable affirms that right living (in the parable, the Kingdom of God) is like a seed that is beginning to grow. The process begins slowly when seeds are planted in the ground. Once the process of growth begins, the seeds have the ability to grow on their own even though they initially do so secretly and their progress is not visible. The parable states we don't know how this growth takes place, but it does.

Those in recovery often doubt that they are making progress. They need to be reminded that "right living" (sobriety) begins when the seeds of a new life are sown. Beginning therapy, participating in a self-help group, etc. are examples of the seeds of recovery being planted. It is common for progress to remain unnoticed even though it is taking place. Nobody knows exactly how this process occurs, but millions have been able to recover once the seeds of sobriety have been planted. Table 7.7, below, outlines the use of the parable.

Progress towards true recovery is often painfully slow. This can be discouraging. The parable of "the Seed Secretly Growing" acknowledges this fact. In spite of delays, however, the seed of recovery may be taking root. This parable deals with these realities and can help people control their impatience.

Table 7.7: "The Seed Growing Secretly": Invisible Progress

Parable	Application	Uses
Seed Growing Secretly	The growth of a program of recovery can be slow. In addition, people often do not understand why recovery is taking place. As a result those seeking recovery can become impatient and/or doubt that progress is taking place. The parable of the "Seed Growing Secretly" can be used to counsel such people.	People may be discouraged and impatient because their progress in recovery is taking so long. The parable can be used to emphasize that growth, although real, may not be overtly obvious. People may not understand how recovery works and, as a result, come to believe it doesn't really exist. This parable can be used to encourage such people
Discussion	The parable of the "Seed Secretly Growing" emphasizes that growth, although real, may not be obvious. Often progress "below the surface" is laying the groundwork for future advances. People should accept this fact and realize that initially change may be slow and invisible.	

Parable # 8: "The Parable of the Tower": *Luke* 14:28–30

When people seek to achieve great things (such as recovering from alcoholism or substance abuse), they need to think about how these tasks will be accomplished. Working towards a difficult goal should not be a random or haphazard process.

"The Parable of the Tower" involves a builder who is constructing a great tower. Jesus reminds the listener that initially calculating the costs is essential. If this is not done, the project may not be completed and the person attempting the venture might be shamed.

Recovering from alcoholism or substance abuse is a monumental task. Many people in recovery affirm that regaining and maintaining sobriety is the most difficult task they have ever pursued. As a result, people seeking recovery need to think about the costs associated with sobriety, not just the benefits. Many people fail at sobriety because they do not come to grips with what they may have to give up in order to remain sober. These costs often involve more than money and material possessions. Old friends and ways of life that are associated with drinking and drugging might have to be abandoned (at least initially and, perhaps, permanently.) The process of gaining true sobriety may take many years. These costs need to be recognized and accepted. If so, recovering people will be better able to accommodate themselves to their new life; when this happens, the odds of recovery are greatly increased.

If people do not recognize the true costs of recovery, they may backslide and further shame themselves because they will not have adequately anticipated what they have to give up and what the costs of recovery really are. A view of the parable is presented in Table 7.8, presented below:

Table 7.8: "The Parable of the Tower": Careful planning can lead to success

Parable	Application	Uses
The Tower	People often need to think about the process of their recovery. Doing so includes acknowledging costs that must be paid, (including how people must transform their lives in order to remain sober.) The "Parable of the Tower" can help people to think about these costs.	When people begin a program of recovery, they need to plan how it will be accomplished and recognize the costs they will have to pay. People involved in recovery may need to periodically reaffirm the price they must pay in order maintain their resolve
Discussion	"The Parable of the Tower" is concerned with planning, acknowledging the costs involved in a decision, and developing an attitude that emphasizes the benefits are worth the price that must be paid. The parable also warns that those who do not recognize and acknowledge the true costs may stumble and not be able to achieve their goals. Dealing with these issues is often an essential part of a program of recovery.	

Recovery doesn't just happen. It takes hard work and planning. It also involves costs and tradeoffs that must be planned for. Those who exert thought and effort are more likely to be successful. "The Parable of the Tower" emphasizes the power of planning and the fact that those who do not plan and think ahead are likely to shame and disappoint themselves.

Parable # 9: "The Parable of the Sower" *Matthew* 13:1–9

The parable of "The Sower" is the story of a farmer who plant seeds. Some of these seeds fall on rocky ground; they quickly sprout, but their roots are eventually dried by the sun and they die. Other seeds are planted among weeds and are crowded out. As a result, they fail. Others are planted in good soil and they grow to be fruitful.

Those seeking sobriety are constantly reminded to avoid making their sobriety vulnerable by associating with people who may trigger a relapse or by visiting places that may tempt the person to drink and/or drug. Programs of sobriety can be viewed in terms of the seeds that are planted in different places. The seeds all have the same potential to develop in fruitful and positive ways, but not all do so. Some are located where they cannot take root so they die. Others find themselves crowded out by weeds.

Those in recovery must give the seeds of their sobriety a fertile place in which to develop and grow. If this does not happen, their sobriety may not mature. The parable can be used to warn people to choose environments that will aid, not undermine, their sobriety.

Presented in tabular form, the parable is portrayed in Table 7.9:

Table 7.9. "The Parable of the Sower": The Power of Circumstances

Parable	Application	Uses
The Sower	Those seeking sobriety, need to "plant" their recovery where it has a chance to succeed. Quickly returning to the haunts and lifestyle that led to substance abuse may choke out sobriety or provide a weak root system that is vulnerable. By planting a program of sobriety within a supportive context (and one with minimal temptations), the chances of sobriety will increase.	When people are beginning a recovery, they strategies that promote success. "The Parable of the Sower" emphasizes that even good seeds will fail if planted in the wrong place. This fact can encourage people to avoid what might undercut success. After relapse, people may become wonder that went wrong. The parable emphasizes that success depends upon a proper environment.
Discussion	"The Parable of the Sower" emphasizes that for good things to grow they need to be located in an appropriate environment. Equally good seeds of sobriety that are planted in different environments will vary in their degree of success. Those seeking recovery need to keep this fact in mind in order to better insure their success. This parable provides a way of addressing this important issue.	

Those in recovery need to live in ways that will not undermine their progress. Unfortunately, these people often hope to quickly resume their previous lives while maintaining sobriety. Attempting to do so, however, may be dangerous. "The parable of The Sower" provides a way to deal with such issues.

Parable # 10 "The Great Pearl" (*Matthew* 13 45–6)

Those who have achieved a successful sobriety often insist that it is their most valuable possession. As a result, these people consciously choose to live in a way that will help them to remain free of drugs and/or alcohol.

The parable of "The Great Pearl" can provide a useful lesson in this regard. The parable concerns a man who found a pearl of great value. In order to possess this treasure he sold all he had in order to buy it. This parable can be used to reinforce one of the key principles of recovery: that sobriety is the most important aspect of life and that anything can justifiably be sacrificed in order to get or maintain it.

Table 7.10 presents the "Parable of the Great Pearl" in an abstracted form:

Table 7.10: "The Great Pearl": The need to abandon all to gain the great gift

Parable	Application	Uses
Great Pearl	Many people may balk at giving up important aspects of their lives in order to gain sobriety. The parable of "The Pearl" helps them to get their priorities in order. The recovering person's most valuable possession is their sobriety. Other things of value will be lost is sobriety it abandoned. Thus, they need to do whatever is necessary in order to get or maintain a sober life in recovery.	People who are beginning a program of recovery may balk at the price they must pay to gain sobriety. By emphasizing the value of sobriety and equating it with the Great Pearl, these people can be encouraged to do whatever is necessary to remain sober. Those who have been sober for a while may be discouraged because of what they have had to give up during their recovery. By equating the Great Pearl with their sobriety, the true value of their recovery can be emphasized.
Discussion	The parable of "The Great Pearl" emphasizes that when something is priceless, people should be willing to give up everything in order to get it. For many recovering people, sobriety is priceless. As a result, they should be willing to sacrifice all in order to get or maintain it.	

"The parable of the Great Pearl" can be used to emphasize the value of sobriety. Doing so is useful when newcomers are planning their program of recovery. It can also be used to encourage people to maintain their resolve.

The Use of Parables in Counseling

This essay has presented discussions regarding how to adapt a sample of the parables of Jesus so that they can help clients deal with and recover from substance abuse. A basic premise underlying this work is that a spiritual and religious heritage often provides the strength and hope that those seeking recovery need if they are to make significant advances in their lives. Those who come from a Christian tradition may find that the *Bible* and its teachings provide such hope, counsel, and positive examples.

When this is true, linking recovery to the comfort and positive example of a religious heritage can be a good and productive strategy. Certainly, doing so is not universally appropriate for all people, but on many occasions religious traditions can be employed as powerful tools of recovery.

There is, however, a profound difference between therapy and evangelical activity. Therapy involves helping distressed people recapture their lives in a self-directed way that reflects who they are and who they want to be. In general, the ethics of the helping professions encourages treating clients in such a manner. I embrace this acid test when evaluating the legitimacy of specific strategies of therapy.

On some occasions, in contrast, a counselor, therapist, or other concerned person (lay or professional) may wish to combine therapy with some kind of religious inculcation. Those who combine counseling with advocating a particular set of religious beliefs can easily expand beyond promoting the goals of the client and, thereby, undercut self-determinism. Although the counselor may sincerely believe that doing so serves the best interests of clients, such actions can easily venture into a pattern of violating the principle that people should be able to control their own destiny and that counselors need to respect their wishes.

Those who are victimized by substance abuse, for example, typically come to therapy at a low ebb in their lives and at a time when it is obvious that the path they have chosen has not worked. Circumstances and their own failed lives might combine to create a situation where their indiscretions have "softened them up" to such a degree that they are susceptible to religious conversion (or can be encouraged to return to the church after an absence.) Faith-based individuals who provide counseling may, under these situations, be tempted to combine therapy and evangelism of a subtle (or not so subtle) nature.

Certainly, those seeking recovery might turn to God in positive, natural, and inevitable way and in a manner that should be embraced and nurtured. On other occasions, in contrast, frightened, shamed, and confused people may be particularly impressionable due to the sorrow, shame, and desperation they face. Some of these people may not, if left to their own devises, be interested in embracing the Christian faith (or a particular version of it.) Due to the events in their lives, however, they may be susceptible to suggestions made by authority figures, such as counselors who are helping them. Thus, those who provide therapy (be they religious leaders, lay practitioners, or those serving in a non-professional capacity) often have great power that they might use in a manipulative way that serves their agendas, not those of the client. Thus, great care needs to be exerted when counselors who possess a strong religious faith deal with clients who may not be truly interested in religious matters.

This is an era in which people in government are debating the appropriateness of providing public money so that faith-based groups can provide services (such as substance abuse counseling.) There are strong arguments in favor of doing so. One reason to favor such programs is that many people are religious and, as a result, they are best served by programs that use their spiritual heritage as tools of recovery. Opponents of providing public money to faith-based social services programs often complain that those who provide counseling may have a dual agenda. On the one hand, they provide services to help the clients achieve their goals (such as gaining sobriety.) At the same time, however, these faith-based programs (or particular people involved with them) may be tempted to interject a religious content in order to convert people. When they venture into such activities, public funding becomes inappropriate.

This chapter has provided advice regarding how to employ the parables of Jesus in substance abuse counseling. It was noted that many people who are familiar with the Christian tradition will be able to respond to these stories in powerful and productive ways, especially when they are presented within the context of therapy. Specific suggestions on how to do so have been provided.

In order for readers to see a practical application of how the parables can be used within the context of substance abuse counseling, a sample treatment plan is provided in the following appendix. It is hoped that the suggestions provided in this paper are useful in helping pastoral counselors to envision appropriate ways to employ the parables in their work.

Those using these tools in a therapeutic manner, however, need to use great care so that religion is used in ways that help clients practice self-determinism. In addition, these programs need to be employed in a manner that insures that not even the smallest appearance of inappropriate evangelical activity can be suggested. While it is understandable that faith-based counselors may hope their clients will experience some sort of religious conversion or revitalization, they need to act in a manner that will shield pastoral counseling from being accused of harboring hidden agendas and working to convert people who are malleable due to the tragedies in their lives.

While recovery and a religious transformation may be linked in a powerful, natural, and productive manner, this will not always be the case. Counselors need to keep this in mind and help people achieve their own chosen destiny, whatever it might be. Faith-based counseling that is employed in an appropriate manner can serve a wide variety and clients and do so in a way that does not violate their right to self-determinism.

Appendix: A Sample Treatment Plan

Treatment Plan for Orientation to Therapy

Presenting Problem: Alcoholic Dependence DSM IV–TR 303.90

By Alf H. Walle (counselor)

Definitions

1. Client exhibits a drinking pattern that can be clinically described as alcoholic.
2. Client states that although he/she wants to stop drinking, he/she has been unable to gain the skills and insights needed to do so.

Goals

1. Make client aware of the seriousness of alcohol abuse Help client develop confidence that he/she can recover.
2. Help client believe it is possible to live a good and fruitful life free of alcohol.
3. Help client gain specific tools needed for recovery.

Interventions

Biblical parables are employed as tools of intervention. The strategy is to use familiar stories typically used for spiritual enlightenment within the context of therapy and self help

This is done is a systematic manner outlined below.

5 WEEK TREATMENT INTERVENTION		
Date	*Objective*	*Interventions*
Session 1	Initial meeting. Help client adjust to and understand treatment. Encourage client by pointing out that even if little progress has been made thus far, recovery can grow in positive and productive ways.	Welcome the client to treatment and go over whatever routine issues need to be discussed. Acknowledge that the client may be discouraged and encourage the client to speak candidly about such issues. Use the "Parable of the Mustard Seed" to underscore that a small amount of hope and resolve can grow to productive strength. Discuss beginning therapy as a seed that has the potential to grow. Probe client as required in order to understand the client's optimism or pessimism. Respond using the metaphor of the mustard seed (and other tools of therapy) as required in order to intervene in helpful ways.
Session 2	Help the client realize that even if no overt signs are visible, progress can still be taking place in subtle and covert ways.	Remind client that progress is typically a slow and steady process. Clients should not expect changes to come quickly or dramatically. Use the "Parable of the Seed Growing Secretly" to underscore this truth. Emphasize that progress might be taking place even if these changes are not overtly obvious. Underscore that internal and invisible progress is the first step of recovery.
Session 3	Help the client to realize that he/she will need to create a strong foundation upon which to build a program of recovery.	In order to achieve a lasting and productive recovery, clients need a strong foundation upon which to build their lives. If clients are impatient, take shortcuts, and do not create this foundation, the potential for relapse may be strong. Use the "Parable of the Wise and Foolish Builders" to emphasize this important point. Having discussed the parable and its message, brainstorm with the client regarding how a strong foundation for recovery can be created.

Session 4	Help the client to realize that a price must be paid in order to achieve and maintain sobriety.	Recovery is hard work and often incurs great costs (in terms of abandoning an old and possibly treasured way of life, friends, etc.) The "Parable of the Tower" will be used to discuss such situations. The parable emphasizes that the costs of a project (in this case recovery) need to be estimated before work starts. A client that does so will have a greater chance of success. After discussing this issue, the counselor and client can analyze the specific costs that this unique person will need to accept for the sake of sobriety.
Session 5	Help the client to realize that he/she will be justified if they truly and humble regret past misdeeds and if they act in a responsible manner in the future. Create a bridge between the now-completed orientation to therapy and their future therapy and self-help efforts. Congratulate the client for completing the orientation.	Clients seeking to recover often have a poor self image. The "Parable of the Pharisee and the Tax Collector" can be used in such situations. The parable emphasizes that people who are truly sorry for their misdeeds and strive to rise above them are justified, while those who show the outward signs of goodness (but lack humility and compassion in their hearts) are not. Having talked about the parable and its message, the client and counselor can discuss building and maintaining a good self image. The session ends with (1) the counselor congratulating the client for completing the orientation to therapy and (2) creating a bridge to the next phase of their recovery.

Each of the parables employed in this treatment plan is analyzed in the paper (above.) Readers are referred to these discussions if they seek fuller details regarding these parables and how they can be applied within the context of therapy.

References

Bailey, K. E. (1976) Poet and Peasant: A Literary Cultural Appraoch to the Parables in Luke (Grand Rapids, Michigan Eerdmas.)

Bailey, K. E. (1980) Through Peasent Eyes: More Lucan Parables (Grand Rapids, Michigan Eerdmas.)

Blomberg (1990), C. L. Interpreting the Parables (Downers Grove, Illinois: Intervarsity.)

Christopher, J (1992) SOS Sobriety: The Proven Alternative to Twelve Step Programs (New York Prometheus Books.)

Christopher, J (1997) How to Stay Sober: Recovery Without Religion (New York Prometheus Books.)

Howarth (1997)

Harris, Marvin (1964) The Nature of Cultural Things (New York: Random House.)

Harris, Marvin (1968) The Rise of Anthropological Theory (New York: Crowell.)

Harris, Marvin (1980) Cultural Materialism: The Struggle for a Science of Culture (New York: Vintage.)

Hultgren, Arland J. (2000) The Parables of Jesus: A Commentary (Grand Rapids, Michigan: William B. Eerdman.)

Jensen, George S. (2000) Storytelling in Alcoholics Anonymous: A Rhetorical Analysis (Carbondale, Illinois: University of Southern Illinois Univeristy.)

Jones, Peter Rhea (1984) Studying the Parables of Jesus (Macon, Georgia: Smyth and Helwys.)

Kirkpatrick, J (1978) Turnabout: Help For a New Life (New York: Doubleday.)

Kirkpatrick, J 1990) Stages of a New Life Program (New York: Doubleday.)

Kistemaker (1989) Trimpey (1985) Rational Recovery For Alcoholics: The Small Book (New York: Dell.

O'Reilly, Edmund (1997) Sobering Tails: Narratives of Alcohol and Recovery (Amherst, Massachusetts: University of Massachusetts Press.)

Pike, Kenneth (1954) Language in Relation to a Unified Theory of the Structure of Human Behavior (Glendale, California: Summer Institute of Linguistics.)

Travis, Trysh (2004) "Print Culture in the AA Fellowship" in *The Social History of Alcohol and Drugs_V. 19* 28–62.)

Walle, Alf . H. (2004) The Path of Handsome Lake: A Model of Recovery For Native People (Greenwich Connecticut: Information Age Publishers.)

Walle, Alf H. (2004a)"Native Americans and Alcoholism Therapy: The Example of Handsome Lake as a Tool of Recovery" *Journal of Ethnicity in Substance Abuse* (Volume 3 # 2 55–79.

Walle, Alf . H. (20070 Recovery the Native Way (Greenwich Connecticut: Information Age Publishers: in press.)

Walle, Alf . H. (2207b) Recovery the Native Way Workbook (Greenwich Connecticut: Information Age Publishers: in press.)

Walle, Alf . H. (2007c) Recovery the Native Way: Therapists' Guide (Greenwich Connecticut: Information Age Publishers: in press.)

Warhol, Robyn R. and Michie, Helena (1996) "Twelve Step Theology: Narratives of Recovery/Recovery as Narrative in Getting a Life: Everyday Uses of Autobiography in Sidonie Smith and Julia Watson, eds. (Minneapolis: University of Minnesota Press.)

Debts Repaid and Leadership Shown

Biblical scholarship takes place both internally and within a larger intellectual community. A basic premise of this book is that to be full and equal partners within the world of ideas, disciplines need to both take what is offered and give back in appropriate and relevant ways. The observation was made that for a variety of understandable reasons, *Biblical* scholarship (in recent generations) seems to have taken more that it is given back. On an optimistic note, the observation was also made that without much effort, *Biblical* scholarship could emerge as a "full partner" within the intellectual world by giving back. Working to achieve that goal has been encouraged.

While all 7 chapters showcase, in various degrees, this dual process of taking and giving, Chapters 6 and 7 were more pointed in that regarding the potential contributions of Biblical scholarship. It is hoped that such examples will provide clues to the reader regarding other ways in which Biblical scholarship can be expanded in a provocative and useful manner that serves others.

Chapter 6 can be envisioned as repaying a debt. Form criticism, a major method of *Biblical* analysis borrowed heavily from scholarly disciplines, such as folklore. As a result, the intellectual "balance sheet" is tipped in that direction. The tools that *Biblical* scholarship has created through this borrowing, however, can be of service the donor disciplines that originally contributed what they had to offer. Chapter 6 demonstrates how *Biblical* scholars can offer aid to the other disciplines, such as folklore, that initially helped them.

In Chapter 7, aspects of the *New Testament* (as well as their analysis by *Biblical* scholars), were presented in a manner that was designed to help alcohol and substance abuse counseling to better accomplish their goals. This is a case of *Biblical* scholarship contributing in ways that extends beyond merely "balancing the score." In this example, *Biblical* scholarship ventures into new areas and uses its expertise to help others do their job in a more appropriate and effective manner. This chapter, furthermore, demonstrates how *Biblical* scholarship can range beyond the ivory tower by participating within the (so called) "real world." By doing so, the scope and influence of

Biblical scholarship can be enhanced and the "other worldly" reputation of the field can be tempered.

This book is the product of one person with a specific background. As a result, few generalities can be gleaned from it. Nonetheless, the case has been made that *Biblical* scholarship is in a position to exert a wider influence than it has in the past. These two chapters are presented as evidence of this potential

Epilogue

Biblical scholarship has been around for many hundreds of years. In that time, it and the broader intellectual community have gone through many changes. Due to these transformations, the position and the status of the field have constantly been evolved.

Early in this collection of essays, I mentioned that in recent generations *Biblical* scholarship appears to have settled into (or been forced to accept) the role of what I called a "recipient discipline" (i.e. an area of study that takes more from other fields than it gives back.) To be a full and contributing part of the academic and intellectual community, however, the flow of borrowing and contributing needs to go in both directions. According to the present arrangement, *Biblical* scholarship risks losing clout, prestige, and influence within the wider world of research, scholarship, and thought.

This short monograph suggests that *Biblical* scholarship clearly has the ability to contribute to the wider intellectual community in broad, varied, unique, and productive ways. This assertion has been backed up with specific examples of how the field has done so in the past and with the prediction that it can do even more in this regard in the future. An idiosyncratic array of my writings showcased a variety of ways in which the field can and should exert an influence beyond its own circumscribed boundaries. No doubt the readers of this book will have their own ideas and perspectives that far outdistance the superficial musings offered here.

Biblical scholarship has a long and impressive history. While it has (and should have) an appropriately circumscribed universe of discourse, the field also has the potential to work within the broader intellectual context by contributing the techniques and perspectives it has learned along the way so others can benefit from them. By doing so, *Biblical* scholarship can help others to achieve their goals.

These accomplishments can be earned without sacrificing the focus and mission that makes *Biblical* scholarship unique. This book is dedicated to all who seek to so while maintaining the historic core of the field.

Index